To　　　　W9-BIM-077　　　ray

from Theressa Crain

FORMATIVE FACTORS
in Christian Character

J. M. PRICE

Convention Press

NASHVILLE, TENNESSEE

Library of Congress Catalog Card Number: 59-14427

Printed in the United States of America
7.5 AT 59 R.R.D.

To the Memory of My Mother

My Finest Example of Christian Character

About the Author

J. M. PRICE was born and reared on a farm near Fair Dealing, Kentucky. He attended the ungraded country school at Maple Springs and was awarded the common school diploma through a county examination. He received the B.S. degree from Western Kentucky State College; the A.B. degree from Baylor University; the A.M. degree from Brown University; and the Th.M., Th.D., and Ph.D. degrees from Southern Baptist Theological Seminary. Baylor conferred on him the LL.D. degree.

Dr. Price attended Sunday school at the Baptist church when it was in session and at the Methodist church at other times. He was converted at fourteen and joined the Pleasant Hope Baptist Church. His public school teaching began at Cleveland School, better known as "Shoo Fly." Later he was principal of the high school at Marlow, Indian Territory. He was pastor in Kentucky, Rhode Island, and Texas—twenty-one years pastor of one country church.

The first salaried associational Sunday school work in the South was done by him in Blood River Association in Kentucky. He was field Sunday school worker in the mountain section of that state, then state Sunday school secretary. He established the School of Religious Education at Southwestern Seminary in 1915 and directed it for forty-one years. Since then he has served as visiting professor and curriculum consultant at Hardin-Simmons University.

Dr. Price is the author of *Christianity and Social Problems, Vital Problems in Christian Living, Jesus the Teacher* (translated into Spanish, Portuguese, and Chinese), and *Mastering Life's Problems.* He served as general editor of *An Introduction to Religious Education, A Program of Religious Education, A Survey of Religious Education, Baptist Leaders in Religious Education, Ten Men from Baylor,* and *Southwestern Men and Messages.*

FORMATIVE FACTORS IN CHRISTIAN CHARACTER is a revision, expansion, and rewriting of his former book *Personal Factors in Character Building.*

Contents

Church Study Course for Teaching and Training

THE CHURCH STUDY COURSE for Teaching and Training began October 1, 1959. It is a merger of three courses previously promoted by the Sunday School Board—the Sunday School Training Course, the Graded Training Union Study Course, and the Church Music Training Course.

The course is fully graded. The system of awards provides a series of five diplomas of twenty books each for Adults or Young People, one diploma of ten books for Young People, two diplomas of five books each for Intermediates, and two diplomas of five books each for Juniors. Book awards earned previously in the Sunday School Training Course, the Graded Training Union Study Course, and the Church Music Training Course may be transferred to the new course.

The course is comprehensive, with books grouped into nineteen categories. The purpose of the course is to (1) help Christians to grow in knowledge and conviction; (2) help them grow toward maturity in Christian character and competence for service; (3) encourage them to participate worthily as workers in their churches; and (4) develop leaders for all phases of church life and work.

The Church Study Course for Teaching and Training is promoted by the Baptist Sunday School Board, 127 Ninth Avenue, North, Nashville, Tennessee, through its Sunday School, Training Union, Church Music, and Church Administration departments, and by these same departments in the states affiliated with the Southern Baptist Convention. A complete description of the course and the system of awards may be found in the *Church Study Course for Teaching and Training* catalog, which may be obtained without charge from any one of these departments.

A record of all awards earned should be maintained in each church. A person should be designated by the church to keep the files. Forms for such records may be ordered from any Baptist Book Store.

Requirements for Credit in Class
or Home Study

IF CREDIT IS desired for the study of this book in a class or by home study, the following requirements must be met:

I. IN CLASSWORK

1. The class must meet a minimum of seven and one-half clock hours. The required time does not include assembly periods. Ten class periods of forty-five minutes each are recommended. (If laboratory or clinical work is desired in specialized or technical courses, this requirement may be met by six clock hours of classwork and three clock hours of supervised laboratory or clinical work.)

2. A class member who attends all class sessions and completes the reading of the book within a week following the last class session will not be required to do any written work.

3. A class member who is absent from one or more sessions must answer the questions on all chapters he misses. In such a case, he must turn in his paper within a week and must certify that the book has been read.

4. The teacher should request an award for himself. When a person teaches a book in sections B, C, or D of any category or conducts an approved unit of instruction for Nursery, Beginner, or Primary children he will be granted an award in category 11, Special Studies, which will count as an elective on his own diploma. He should specify in his request the name of the book taught, or the unit conducted for Nursery, Beginners, or Primaries.

5. The teacher should complete the Request for Book Award—Class Study (Form 150) and forward it within two weeks after the completion of the class to the Church Study Course Awards Office, 127 Ninth Avenue, North, Nashville 3, Tennessee.

II IN HOME STUDY

1. A person who does not attend any class session may receive credit by answering all questions for written work as indicated in the book. When a person turns in his paper on home study, he must certify that he has read the book.

2. Students may find profit in studying the text together, but

individual papers are required. Carbon copies or duplicates in any form cannot be accepted.

3. Home study work papers may be graded by the pastor or a person designated by him, or they may be sent to the Church Study Course Awards Office for grading. The form Request for Book Award—Home Study (Form 151) must be used in requesting awards. It should be mailed to Church Study Course Awards Office, 127 Ninth Avenue, North, Nashville 3, Tennessee.

III. CREDIT FOR THIS BOOK

This book is No. 1743 in category 17, section A.

Suggested Audio-Visual Materials

For Use in Teaching This Book

ANY OF THE following motion pictures or filmstrips can be used to present problems in character development that will provide laboratory situations in which to apply the teachings of this book. Otherwise, they should only be used as extra curriculum materials.

Motion Pictures:

A Job or Calling
Return to Faith
Their Future Is Yours
Formula for Failure
Choose Ye This Day
With His Help

Filmstrips:

Know Your Child Series:
Sources of Truth, Part I
The Dynamics of Growth, Part II
The Stages of Growth (Early) Part III
The Stages of Growth (Later) Part IV
Similarities of Growth, Part V
Freedom and Discipline in Growth, Part VII
Family Give and Take
Family Togetherness

CHAPTER 1

I. THE FACT OF HEREDITY

1. Biblical Emphasis
2. Historical Evidence
3. General Observation

II. THE SCOPE OF HEREDITY

1. Biological Aspects
2. Prenatal Influences
3. Social Inheritance

III. THE UTILIZATION OF HEREDITY

1. Recognize Heredity's Influence on Life
2. Realize that Education Modifies Heredity
3. Regard Heritage as Character Material
4. Know the Pupil's Previous Background
5. Seek to Restrain Harmful Tendencies
6. Strive to Cultivate Good Traits

1

Hereditary Tendencies

THE PUPIL DOES NOT COME into the hands of the teacher like a blank sheet of paper. Rather he is more nearly like the ancient scroll on which a number of things have been overwritten from time to time. To use the imagery of Oliver Wendell Holmes, "We are the omnibuses in which our ancestors ride." Inherited traits form an important part of the pupil's make-up and provide much of the raw material for character. An understanding of the hereditary background of the pupil is therefore very important. Someone has said that to guide the pupil properly we should start with his grandparents. We cannot do this, but we do need to know something of what they contributed if we are to have a working understanding of the characteristics and potentialities of the pupil.

There have been varying views on the importance of heredity. Some have felt that heredity is the main factor in human personality. Luther Burbank, the plant wizard, went so far as to say that twelve picked families under ideal conditions could accomplish more for the race in ten generations than would be done in a thousand years under ordinary conditions. This is an extreme emphasis. John B. Watson, a prominent psychologist, went to the other extreme, practically denying the influence of inborn tendencies. He indicated that he could take twelve healthy infants at random and by the proper environment and training make of each of them anything he desired, regardless of talents, tendencies, abilities, or other inheritances. This view also is radical. The truth is somewhere between these two extremes.

I. THE FACT OF HEREDITY

Is heredity a reality? Are there facts that establish it? The answers to these questions are most important as we approach the subject. Let us look first at some of the evidences for the significance of heredity as a factor in character formation.

1. Biblical Emphasis

On heredity, as on other matters of importance, the Bible has something to say. It indicates, as the catechism said, "In Adam's fall we sinned all," and the entire race has inherited the evil effects. Moses spoke of God as "visiting the iniquity of the fathers upon the children unto the third and fourth generation" (Ex. 20:5). Jeremiah said: "Our fathers have sinned . . . ; and we have borne their iniquities" (Lam. 5:7). "The fathers have eaten a sour grape, and the children's teeth are set on edge" (Jer. 31:29). Very definitely the Bible indicates the harmful effects of inheritance.

But the results may be on the good side of the ledger as well as on the bad. Samuel, the great judge, had the remarkable Hannah for his mother. The brilliant Solomon had the renowned David for his father. Paul came of blue-blooded, Jewish Pharisee stock. And Timothy had the rich background of his mother Eunice and grandmother Lois. So, inheritance has its good as well as its bad side. By precept and example the Bible stresses both aspects. Heredity is very clearly and unmistakably a Bible teaching.

2. Historical Evidence

History also bears evidence to the reality and significance of heredity. A striking instance is found in the early twenty-one hundred descendants of the five Jukes sisters in New York state, whose history for over a century has been studied. More than one out of eight died in infancy; nearly a third were feeble-minded, and about 40 per cent were paupers, criminals, or prostitutes. Fewer than 1 per cent learned a trade, half of these learning it in prison, and not one became a common school graduate or a soldier. The family cost the state over two and a half million dollars. Similar were the descendants of Martin Kallikak, a soldier, and a feeble-minded girl by whom he had an illegitimate son. About one sixth of the offspring of this son died in infancy, nearly a third were feeble-minded, and about a fifth were illegitimate, immoral, or alcoholic.

On the other hand, the descendants of Martin Kallikak and a Quaker girl of a good family whom he married later were practically all normal. Only about 3 per cent died in infancy, and practically none were immoral, epileptic, or criminal. This record is quite a contrast to that of his first line of offspring.

More outstanding are the 1,396 descendants of Johnathan Edwards, a famous minister and college president. There was not a pauper or criminal among them. On the other hand there were 295 college graduates, 100 lawyers, 100 or more ministers and missionaries, 75 army officers, 60 or more authors, 60 physicians, and 13 college presidents.

The offspring of John Sebastian Bach, the famous organist and composer, included in six generations, fifty-seven musicians of repute, twenty-nine especially outstanding. Heredity does have its influence, particularly when the social aspect is included.

3. General Observation

All of us have observed that persons come into life with certain characteristics which mark them off from others. These traits include such matters as color, height, shape of face, size of head, glands, instincts, intelligence, and other characteristics. It is readily observable that no two people are exactly alike, and the things that mark the differences are matters of heredity. In fact, the points in common are also matters of inheritance. Often we can recognize a youth because of the likeness to his father or mother. These differences and similarities are observable by all in the laboratory of life.

It does not require any special ability or scientific training to recognize inherited traits in people. "Like father like son" is a saying almost as old as the race, and it is based on observable characteristics. Of course the trained person will be able to detect differences the untrained eye will be unable to see, but all of us observe readily the similarities and differences due to inheritance. They stand out on the very surface of things. The limits within which development takes place are very largely determined by heredity, since it includes intellectual ability, emotional capacity, and general possibilities. Blood always tells.

II. THE SCOPE OF HEREDITY

Considered in the broad sense, heredity, or inheritance, covers quite a wide range. We shall notice briefly several phases. Other aspects might be considered, but these will indicate the significance of the matter for the teacher.

1. *Biological Aspects*

The first and most evident phase of inheritance is the biological aspect. This, with all of its potentialities for good or bad, is determined by the union of the two parent cells including all that is latent in them. S. S. Sargent says:

> We inherit the color of our eyes, hair, and skin; shape of skull and a tendency to be short or tall. Certain physical defects like color-blindness, stub fingers and some forms of baldness are inherited. No common diseases except diabetes are hereditary, though inherited pre-dispositions toward cancer, tuberculosis, and allergies may exist. Feeble-mindedness is inherited.[1]

Heredity then, imposes certain limitations on life development and determines certain conditions of which the individual needs to be aware and to which he needs to learn to adjust if he is to face life properly. Also, the more completely a teacher understands the inherited limitations and possibilities of the pupil, the more intelligently can that teacher guide the pupil in learning to use his powers to the fullest extent, in line with God's plan for his life.

It is generally accepted that acquired characteristics are not inherited. "The blacksmith's offspring does not possess a large right biceps, nor the child of the Flathead Indian a misshapen skull. . . . No child is 'born a musician,' 'a doctor,' 'a minister,' or 'a bad boy.'"[2] Muscles, nerves, instincts, glands, brain texture, and other elements are inherited, as are race, sex, family characteristics, and the possibilities of growth.

So the fabric out of which Christian character is made is largely inherited. Biological heredity sets limits beyond which we cannot go in the development of life. In general it furnishes raw material for Christian character. It is important, then, that the young person consider the background of the one he is to marry, and that the government require physical, if not mental, examination before issuing a marriage license. And the teacher needs to know the pupil's hereditary background in order to teach properly.

2. Prenatal Influences

During the months following the union of the parent cells, before a baby is born, its close relation to the body of the mother makes it possible for certain effects to be produced that can affect greatly its life. On this Dr. Stewart F. Cole says:

> The expectant mother's condition of health is extremely important. The quality of the blood stream flowing between her and the fetus predetermines the constitutional ruggedness of the infant. . . . Alcoholism, drugs, the toxin of syphilis may arrest the development of the organism. An unbalanced diet

weakens the vitality. . . . During a heightened sense of fear, anger, or nervousness, adrenalin secretions enter the blood which permit serious, disorganized reactions of the person. . . . Good food, regular rest, moderate exercise, will insure golden returns for her child.[3]

It is evident, then, that apart from strictly biological heredity, or the product of the union of the parent cells, other physical effects result prior to birth that have much to do with the life of the child. It is at this point that venereal disease, also nicotine, alcohol, and other narcotics in the life of the parent, especially the mother, can have harmful effects on the unborn infant.

Dr. H. H. Tidswell of the Royal College of Surgeons in England reports that the rate of mortality per 1,000 children of nonsmokers is 153; the rate for smokers is 227. Because of the vital relation sustained, cigarette-smoking mothers may particularly harm the unborn child. There is some evidence that smoking may contribute to sterility, if we accept the indications of investigations in this field.

A comparison of ten families of drinkers with ten sober families showed that only 10 of 57 of the former were normal, 25 died in infancy, 7 were idiotic, 5 dwarfed, 5 epileptic, and one had St. Vitus's Dance. In the ten sober families 50 were normal, 5 died in infancy, 2 were slightly deformed, 2 backward, 2 had St. Vitus's Dance, and not one was idiotic. Considerable blindness and some feeble-mindedness have been caused by venereal diseases.

3. Social Inheritance

Closely related to biological heredity, and especially to prenatal influence, is social inheritance. By this is meant those influences which the child gets from its environment before it is capable of deliberation and conscious choice. Just as our ancestors transmit to us their race, shape, color of hair, and other physical characteristics, so also they transmit institutions, customs, viewpoints, and prejudices. These are taken over, unconsciously to a large extent, and become a part of our heritage. Social inheritance is the body of traditions, customs, laws, institutional forms, economic impulses, and ethical ideals accumulated through the past ages. This is a rather big dose. It is inheritance, since it is the attainment of the fathers handed on to the children. And it is hereditary in that the child cannot escape it. As he grows in body by absorbing light and air, so he grows in mind by absorbing the mental atmosphere in which he lives. A person is definitely affected by the outstanding characteristics of the environmental area in which he develops his personality.

As indicated, this area includes *points of view*. Whether a person becomes a Baptist or a Methodist, Democrat or Republican, prohibitionist or antiprohibitionist, depends largely on the atmosphere in which he grows up. One gets from his environment many of his views on the sabbath, liquor, and other matters, without ever having considered their merits or demerits. Styles, manners, and customs are acquired this way. Many views that we think are our own have come from our parents, companions, or the general environment. Comparatively few individuals can give very adequate reasons for the particular denominational faith they hold, or for belonging to a certain political party. They have simply inherited a certain point of view.

Attitudes as well as viewpoints are a part of one's social inheritance. Likes and dislikes, loves and hates, sympathies and antipathies, come largely from one's environment. Most loyalties originate this way. People in the North and in the South do not feel the same on racial matters. Baptists and Methodists do not have the same attitude toward immersion. In the mountains of Kentucky, the children from opposing families in the feuds used to want to fight each other on the school playground. Most of our prejudices arise from the environment. Social, religious, and racial difficulties come largely from attitudes carried over, unconsciously, from one generation to the next. We cannot escape our environment.

Forms of response are likewise a part of social inheritance. Children not only think and feel as others do, but also act like them. A study revealed that 85 per cent of kittens that had watched their mothers kill rats did so after four months, while none of those that had been raised up to play with rats killed them. As with kittens, so with people. Children accustomed to seeing their parents drink liquor will likely drink. Studies show that smoking is much more prevalent among children of smoking parents than among children of non-smokers.

During a revival meeting the writer talked to a Junior boy about becoming a Christian. He got no response. It was learned that, although his mother, sisters, grandmothers, and aunts were Christians, the boy's father, brothers, grandfathers, and uncles were not. The boy did religiously as the men did and not as the women desired.

It is evident that social inheritance exerts a great influence over one's life. Although much of Moses' life was under a pagan environment, he never got away from his Hebrew heritage and his mother's teaching. Paul reminded Timothy of "the unfeigned faith that is in thee, which dwelt first in thy grandmother Lois, and thy mother Eunice" (2 Tim. 1:5). Much of the results in the Jukes and Edwards families, previously mentioned, were probably due to social inheritance. It is easier to climb upward if the hands of previous generations reach down from the heights to pull us up than if they reach up from the depths to pull us down. Yet social heredity cannot transmute "leaden instincts" into "golden deeds." Environment and culture are limited.

III. The Utilization of Heredity

The question naturally arises as to the significance of heredity for the teacher. What can he do about it? How can he lay hold of it to the best advantage? There are a number of different ways in which he can utilize it.

1. *Recognize Heredity's Influence on Life*

In the light of what has just been said, we need to realize as teachers that the pupils who come to us are not the unbiased, open-minded creatures we often consider them to be. Rather, they have already been largely fashioned by the viewpoints, attitudes, and activities to which they have been subjected. These inheritances will largely make or mar them, if left alone. Ruja, after studying many orphan children, concluded that their differences corresponded mainly to the differences among their parents, even though the children had been separated from their parents since soon after birth. They resembled their real parents in intelligence more than their foster parents. He concluded: "Heredity in part provides the equipment with which the human organism operates, and hence contributes to determining its level of efficiency." [4] We cannot completely swim away from the blood stream.

So each individual has a bent and bias of his own. Some are normal physically, mentally, and morally, and others are more or less abnormal. All of these individual differences enter into character.

> The first and most fundamental source of character lies within the individual himself. His original capacities in the physical and mental realms form the ground upon which the superstructure of personality must be built. These capacities may be great or small, many or few, shallow or deep, but whatever the range, they set definitely at the beginning of life the limits which the individual will be able to reach in the field of character. [5]

The influence of heredity must be clearly realized. The first step toward the making of character is the recognition of beginnings already made. The teacher must be alert to background conditions in the life of the pupils, particularly his social inheritance, and prepare to teach in a way to help the pupil to build on that which is desirable in his heritage and to overcome that which is undesirable.

2. *Realize that Education Modifies Heredity*

It would be most unfortunate if a look at the influence of heredity left one with a feeling of hopelessness. Rather we should take E. J. Chave's viewpoint: "The limitations set by heredity for an individual and for the race are real boundaries, but within these boundaries there are limitless opportunities for personality development." [6] The emphasis on heredity has been made here to help us realize that something needs to be done and can be done. Nurture can change nature and give one a new lease on life. Benjamin Kidd was right when he said that by inculcating in youth a passion for the ideal we could create a new earth in a single generation. Here is both the teacher's task and his supreme opportunity.

History is filled with illustrations of what can be done with people of intemperate or immoral background through proper cultural processes. Some years ago T. J. Barnardo, after taking 60,000 waifs from the worst surroundings, giving them encouraging suggestions, and putting them in a helpful environment, nurtured 98 per cent of them into good citizens. He said that he had never known a case where the rescue was accomplished early enough and where the training was thorough and continued sufficiently long, in which there occurred a definite reversion to some ancestral badness.

Ziemer in his remarkable book *Education for Death* shows how the leaders in Germany developed a nation of one mind through an educative process. The same could be said of Russia in more recent years. Much more, then, can conversion and Christian training overcome natural weakness, and prejudice. This modifiableness constitutes the hope of, and the challenge to, religious education—both that which precedes and that which follows the experience of the new birth.

3. *Regard Heritage as Character Material*

Too often teachers have thought of their task as that of teaching lessons. In other words they have a material-centered emphasis. They are concerned primarily with getting over to the pupil a body of facts. However, after more careful thought, in recent years this idea has been changed. We have come to realize that we do not teach lessons, we teach people. The lesson material is merely a means to an end. Even the Bible is such, for the very verse of Scripture that asserts inspiration states that its purpose is for instruction, correction, and reproof "that the man of God may be perfect" (2 Tim. 3:16-17). In other words, the Bible gives a life-centered stress. "I don't teach Latin, I teach boys" was the Latin professor's way of putting it. Jesus said he came that people might have life.

In the light of this approach of meeting needs, it is very evident that an understanding of heredity plays a prominent part in the teacher's work. Heritage is indeed the raw material he uses in helping to transform very human persons into worthwhile characters. It is his stock in trade, the warp and woof out of which he is to weave the garment of character. His task is not to hurl truths at a class, but rather to guide each pupil through teaching and environment to a better life. This is done in the light of the background of each one. The teacher must recognize that character is made out of the appetites, attitudes, and ideals. In fact, conversion itself is very largely the supernatural transformation of these human elements. Regeneration is not something apart from life, but the reworking of these innate materials into the fabric of Christian character.

4. *Know the Pupil's Previous Background*

All that has been said points to the need for the Sunday school teacher to know as much as possible about the inheritance of the pupil. What are his parents, brothers, and sisters like? Do they swear, drink, or gamble? Are they churchgoing people? What evil habits has the pupil taken over from his home environment? Does he come from a broken home? These and many other matters need to be known about the pupil if the teacher is to be able to work with him to the best advantage. They are matters that authorities who deal with juvenile delinquents are looking into, and it is being found that most delinquents come from homes that are lacking in one or more areas of desirable background. If a boy's father is a drunkard or libertine, that fact gives the teacher a clue as to things to be stressed. Prejudices, dishonesty, irreligion, and other matters should be known if one is to meet the needs of his pupils most effectively.

In order to know these things, the teacher should visit in the home, observe, talk with the parents, and find out firsthand everything possible. It is also good to talk with the pupil's schoolteacher and schoolmates. And it is helpful to know what his amusements are—the kinds of shows attended, television scenes witnessed, radio programs listened to, and the kind of comics and books read. Also, it is well to be on the alert to detect the manifestation of undesirable traits in class and elsewhere. L. P. Leavell told of a Sunday school teacher who kept what she called a "Class Account Book" in which she jotted down information regarding her pupils, to be used in her preparation of each lesson.

Any teacher will profit by such a plan. The initial step is to secure all the information included in the teacher's record book in the Six Point Record System. Building on this beginning, constantly add information secured from parents, fellow teachers, associates, and personal observation.

5. Seek to Restrain Harmful Tendencies

As undesirable traits show up in the life of the pupil, it is important to do whatever can be done to curb their development and replace them with better ones. This redirection is what the children's workers in Sunday school do through activity teaching. If a child is selfish and unwilling to share toys, the teacher seeks to develop the spirit of sharing. If he has a tendency to lord it over others, the teacher tries to develop the co-operative spirit. The same principle applies regarding the desire for display. The principle operates in relation to other problems, and throughout the other age groups. Selfishness and greed should be curbed, as should tendencies to dishonesty, intemperance, immorality, and other evils. By watching constantly, the teacher may discover such traits early and nip them in the bud. Here is where discipline and restraint come in. "As the twig is bent, the tree is inclined."

This restraint is, of course, achieved in different ways. Building ideals of honesty, purity, temperance, and the like, will help greatly. Developing attitudes along these lines will carry the restraint a step further. Using the public sentiment of the class has a definite value. Denying privileges to those who are disobedient will have its effects.

Children of intemperate or immoral parents should be led to develop an antipathy toward such things. Those from non-Christian and nonchurched homes should be brought to a profession of faith and enjoyable church membership. The social and recreational program of the church has a definite value, especially in keeping youth from harmful places. The Sunday school and Training Union have done much to develop a churchgoing habit and to substitute wholesome for harmful associations.

6. *Strive to Cultivate Good Traits*

It is at least as important to ingrain good ideas, feelings, and habits as it is to eliminate or forestall bad ones. This is Christ's emphasis in the parable of the unclean spirit which returned after being driven out, and on finding the house

empty, repossessed it (Matt. 12:43–45). By developing
ideals, attitudes, and responses, character can be built that
will enable the individual to stand up against harmful environmental influences. That was the experience of Walter
Athearn, who had been taught that no Athearn had ever
used tobacco. So when schoolmates sought to pressure him
into using it, he resisted them successfully. It was by a positive approach that a juvenile delinquent was brought to
Christian experience, church membership, and a useful life
through interest in the creative activities of a Vacation
Bible school. An ounce of prevention is still worth a pound
of cure.

New interests and desires should be carefully cultivated.
Many lives have been made over in this way. A group of
Junior boys, who were headed in a dangerous direction, became intensely interested in the life and teachings of Christ
when a study of these things was involved in making an elec-
trical map of Palestine as a class project. This new interest
tied them on more closely both to the Sunday school and to
Christ.

There is definite value in the procedures advocated by our
children's workers involving the use of many types of activity as an approach to teaching. This plan makes it possible
to employ various natural interests of the child as avenues
for experiencing religious truths in settings which give meaning to the concepts being learned.

Many a boy has been saved from waywardness through
his interest in Boy Scout work. In fact, there are probably
fewer delinquents among Scouts than among any other comparable group. Church camps and RA and GA work have a
distinct value. The Sunday school can be our greatest antidote
against crime and immorality. It has had much to do with
our increase in church membership and in giving. Always we
shall seek to bring the power of Christ into the life of man.
Training as well as teaching is needed to crystallize character.

SUGGESTIONS FOR CLASS DISCUSSION

1. Give other Scripture passages emphasizing the influence of heredity.
2. Which is more powerful, biological heredity or social inheritance? Why?
3. Cite several instances from observation showing how education modifies heredity.
4. What is most important to know about a pupil's background?

---

[1] S. S. Sargent, *The Basic Teachings of the Great Psychologists* (New York: The New Library, 1944), p. 61. Used by permission of Doubleday & Co., Inc., copyright owners.

[2] Stewart G. Cole, *Character Through Christian Education* (Nashville: Abingdon Press, 1946), pp. 31–32.

[3] *Ibid.*, p. 34.

[4] Harry Ruja, *Psychology for Life* (New York: McGraw-Hill Book Co., Inc., 1935), p. 163. Used by permission.

[5] McElhinney and Smith, *Personality and Character Development* (Winona Lake, Indiana: Light and Life Press, 1942), p. 124.

[6] E. J. Chave, *Personality Development in Children* (Chicago: The University of Chicago Press, 1937), p. 45.

CHAPTER 2

I. NATURE OF URGES

II. KINDS OF URGES
1. Preservation
2. Reproduction
3. Social
4. Power
5. Unification

III. CHARACTERISTICS OF URGES
1. Develop Gradually
2. Meet Needs
3. Neither Good nor Bad
4. May be Modified
5. Not Totally Suppressed

IV. SIGNIFICANCE OF URGES
1. Awaken Interests
2. Stimulate Activities
3. Become Storm Centers
4. Develop into Character
5. Need to be Understood
6. Require the Proper Guidance

2

Instinctive Urges

Along with general hereditary tendencies in the life of the person, there are certain more specific inner urges, or drives, that are very significant. In fact, out of them very largely develops character—good or bad. These urges clamor for expression and call for consideration. They constitute a vital part of the raw material of life, and are at the heart of the formation of character. It is very important that teachers understand them and know something about how to deal with them. Very largely, these drives make or mar life, according to the direction given them.

I. NATURE OF URGES

In the early days of psychological treatises instinct was the term that was used for the inner urge or drive, and it was considered a fixed and formal thing. William James, the famous psychologist, defined it as "the faculty of acting in such a way as to produce certain ends without foresight of the ends, and without previous education in the performance." Instinct was considered to be a pattern of response as well as an urge to activity. Early writers put great emphasis on instincts and went much into detail as to their number and significance.

In recent years there has been considerable change in thinking. It has been felt that the term "instinct" is fitted to such matters as a bird's nest-building, but carries too much the idea of a fixed pattern of response to be applicable to human beings who can think and decide. While recognizing

17

the element of urge, modern thought has rejected the hard and fast idea of an instinctive pattern of response.

So instead of the term "instinct" there has been substituted "tendency," "urge," or "drive." These terms carry the idea of inner constraint without suggesting a fixed way of responding, and so are terms more applicable to free moral agents. However, in shifting terminology we have mainly rid ourselves of a mechanistic definition which did not belong with the idea of instinct in the first place. George B. Cutten well says:

> It has been most interesting to see instinct thrown out the front door with a great deal of noise and publicity, and then later stealthily drawn back in the back door disguised and re-named.[1]

In this discussion we are using the word "urge" as the basic noun, and "instinctive" as the qualifying adjective. The term instinctive suggests a stiring to action, and the term urge indicates a certain compulsive element. Each word, to a degree, reinforces the other.

II. KINDS OF URGES

There is no uniformity in the classification of these inner urges. Some psychologists reduce them to three, and others find more than a score. In presenting the following we are simply selecting the basic ones. Fear, hate, love, anger, jealousy, and the like are considered emotional accompaniments of instincts rather than instincts themselves. As Shand says: "When opposed it [the instinct] tends to arouse anger; when satisfied, joy; when frustrated, sorrow; and when it anticipates frustrations, fear." [2] We are dealing here with the instincts themselves rather than with their emotional accompaniments.

1. *Preservation*

As the term indicates, this urge is an inner compulsion to preserve life. It has been referred to as the first law of life, and is possibly the strongest of all drives because of its biological basis. It leads to providing food, clothing, and shelter and "laying up for a rainy day." Savings accounts, insurance, and Social Security are outcomes of the urge for preservation. Satisfying this urge can lead to the acquisition of all kinds of conveniences and extravagances—even two automobiles and a boat. Much of our material progress has grown out of this drive.

This urge helps to account for many of the evils of the day. A person will flee or fight to protect his life. He will, in many cases, steal before he will starve and commit murder before he will see himself or his family's life endangered. Covetousness and greed grow out of this urge. Selfishness is the personification of it. Miserliness, monoply, and unfair competition are extreme results of the urge for preservation. Politicians appeal to this drive to get votes. Well did Jesus say: "Beware of covetousness" (Luke 12:15), and "Whosoever will save his life shall lose it" (Matt. 16:25).

2. *Reproduction*

The reproductive urge has to do with the propagation of the race. It includes the sex and parental drives. In strength it comes along with the preservative. The reproductive urge develops in early adolescence and continues far on into life. It has a strong biological basis as well as a social element. This drive brings the opposite sexes together in courting, mating, and parenthood. Love, unselfishness, and sacrifice grow out of it. It leads to the making of the home, care of the young, and developing the tender emotions of parenthood. The reproductive drive can be one of the most elevating and enriching influences in life or one of the most debasing forces with which an individual must deal.

Since this drive, like the preservative, has a biological as well as a social basis, it can be one of the most difficult to control. Especially is this true when it is accentuated by suggestive literature, movies, and television. Dancing, scanty dress, and suggestive advertising stimulate the reproductive urge. When satisfying it comes to be an end in itself and the mere gratification of physical desire, this drive can be one of the most debasing influences, as we see in the widespread immorality and illegitimacy today. Just as life comes to its highest in parenthood, so it reaches its lowest in unrestrained immorality. Character is definitely debased by wrong use of the reproductive urge.

Jesus' words, "Blessed are the pure in heart" (Matt. 5:8), although not limited to one area of life, certainly include the standard for right control of the reproductive drive.

3. Social

The gregarious disposition is universal. Insects go in groups, birds in flocks, animals in herds, and human beings in crowds. This social urge develops early and runs throughout life. Children play together, youth go in gangs, young men and women have socials, and adults form clubs. People are not satisfied to be alone. This social disposition forms the basis for fellowship and sympathy. In college it results in fraternities; in social life, in civic clubs; and in church work, in classes and groups. It is one of the strongest drives of life. Men do not live by bread alone, but by fellowship with, and the regard of, their fellow men.

The social tendency includes the desire to be with people, to be recognized by them, and to be approved. The normal person wants to be with others at least part of the time. He likes to be noticed and will do extreme things to get recognition. A little child, craving the attention of her companions but unable to do the stunts they did, finally said, "Do you want to see me do something, kids?" Then she jumped six inches from the step to the sidewalk. The craving for approval can lead to pride, rivalry, and jealousy. Vain display is an outgrowth of it. Probably the most common sins among Christian people are in the area of social urges.

Jesus was admonishing his followers to bring their social urges under God's control when he said, "Blessed are the meek [disciplined]" (Matt. 5:5).

4. *Power*

Another very strong and sometimes dangerous tendency is the projective or power drive. It is the disposition to project oneself into the life of persons and things around. It is shown in the activity of childhood, the independence of youth, and the creative and inventive tendencies later. Self-dependence, assertiveness, and aggressiveness grow out of the power drive. There would be little progress without it. Given too much rein, it results in harm. The industrialist may become a monopolist, the civic leader a dictator, and even the religious worker an overlord.

This craving for power can be the cause of much distress and suffering, as we see in countries controlled by dictators. It can cause trouble in democratic countries if monopolists exercise control in industry—whether capital or labor unions—at the expense of others and to their hurt. Among youngsters the power drive leads to bullying and domination and among older persons to conquest and control. Nothing is much more important than that one be able to stand on his own feet and make his own contribution, but nothing is much worse than dominating others and handicapping their freedom.

5. *Unification*

In the human being there is a craving which is not and cannot be found in lower orders of creation. It is the yearning for rational and moral unity, or oneness. It is the desire that standard and practice, or conscience and conduct, harmonize. Otherwise one is unable to live with himself. Either his practice must conform to his standard, or he will change his standard to conform to his practice. One cannot be permanently divided. This fact applies to his relation to others and to God as well as to himself. It is possible that, if the urge for unification is not regarded, there will result the divided self, or cleavage in consciousness, with all of its disturbing results. Continued conflict may lead to drinking to escape from oneself. In fact, lack of inner unification is probably the cause of much drunkenness. In extreme cases, nervous breakdown or insanity may result. We have now more mental patients in our hospitals than those physically ill, and some of the mental sickness is due to inability to reach inner unity.

The secret of such unification is found in the words of Jesus: "Seek ye first the kingdom of God, and his righteousness" (Matt. 6:33). "No man can serve two masters" (Matt. 6:24).

In addition to these various instinctive urges that have been discussed in this chapter, there are a number of other strong tendencies, which have been mentioned from time to time, such as curiosity, inquisitiveness, imitation, conformity, display, pugnacity. However, they are largely the manifestation of instinctive urges, rather than the instincts themselves. For example, curiosity is a manifestation of the projective urge; display, of the social tendency; and pugnacity, of the power drive. Imitation and conformity tie in closely with the urge for unification. Every normal person wants to be in harmony with others. One of our greatest problems is to harmonize and unify these conflicting urges. To help achieve this harmony is one of the most important tasks of the teacher.

III. CHARACTERISTICS OF URGES

There are several things that characterize these instinctive tendencies or drives which we need to realize if we are to understand the individual as we should and deal with him as we ought. To some extent we have noted these characteristics already, but there are other traits that deserve attention.

1. Develop Gradually

Not all of the innate urges or drives are evident at birth or for some time afterward. This fact is very helpful, for the individual would not be able to handle them all at once. It is much better that they appear gradually. By that means they can be woven into the fabric of character. Somewhat like the limbs on a tree, various urges come out and develop more nearly one at a time than en masse. The gang spirit, for example, is not evident in early childhood, but appears in the latter part of this period. Other urges are dominant at different times.

Nor do instinctive urges reach full fruition immediately on appearance. In other words, they do not appear in full bloom. Their gradual development has its advantages. It makes it possible for the individual to be dealt with as an unfolding person rather than as a fixed character. Aims, materials, and methods must be adapted accordingly. Hence the necessity for the age-group approach in church work. Each new, budding interest and power must be dealt with at the opportune time and rightly related to Christ if the individual is to grow into a well-rounded and symmetrical Christian character.

2. Meet Needs

Instinctive urges are not mere blind forces reaching out aimlessly into the dark. Rather, they tend toward things necessary in the life of the individual. They are given for a purpose. The preservative drive seeks to conserve life; the sex and parental, to propagate the race; the social, to relate to others; the projective, to bring achievement; and the integrative, to give unity. All are necessary in the life of the individual. Man would be rather helpless without them. In fact, one could almost say: "Out of the instinctive drives are the issues of life." They are just that nearly central in character building.

It is our business, then, as teachers to do what we can to see that these drives carry people in the direction of what is best. Emphasis on hell ties in with the self-preservative tendency. The same is true of the appeal through rewards. Much of Jesus' teaching relates to the fundamental instinctive drives. In emphasizing meekness, he was seeking to lead away from the danger of the social urge. In stressing peacemaking, he was aiming at the control of the power drive. And in magnifying purity of heart, he was warning against the misuse of the reproductive function. Guiding instinctive drives is at the heart of our task.

It is not enough to lead our pupils to an abstract recognition that Christ is to be the Lord of their lives and the Holy Spirit is to direct their motives and actions. We must help them, in respect to each emerging instinctive drive, to see the direction it must take if the life is to conform to God's plan and purpose.

3. Neither Good nor Bad

These inherited tendencies are neither essentially sinful nor righteous in themselves. They are a necessary part of human equipment and may be used either for good or bad. The end toward which the drive is directed and the motive that controls it determine the rightness or wrongness. Whether or not fighting is good or bad depends on the worthiness of the cause and the necessity for fighting. People should be led to fight against social evils. Sex tendencies are necessary for the propagation of the race, but may be perverted to sinful gratification. Seeking social approval is good if it does not degenerate into a race for popularity.

So neither the doctrine that "nature is right" and must be given free rein nor the other extreme that we are "as bad as we can be and getting worse all the time" is true. As indicated, the rightness or wrongness depends on the end to which the drive is directed and the motive that controls it. Neither the idea that there is no good in instinctive drives nor that they are always right is correct. We must steer clear of the extreme both of the flaunting libertine and the radical ascetic. This concept necessitates giving direction as teachers for the proper use of inner drives and helping pupils to develop the appropriate, controlling motives.

4. *May be Modified*

Drives are not fixed patterns of response. Rather, they are tendencies, or stimuli to action, and may be expressed in various ways. Detailed actions are not implicit in drives. For example, the urge for self-preservation may find its expression in hard work, begging, or stealing. Unused tendencies are liable to shrivel and die. A little chicken placed on a glass floor during the first part of its life will, after a time, cease to scratch. There is sound psychology in the biblical teaching that one may sin away his day of grace, or have his talent taken from him. "Ephraim is joined to idols: let him alone" (Hos. 4:17).

The fact that drives are modifiable constitutes a hope and a warning. It also suggests the importance of being alert. In fact, it indicates that their guidance is one of the most important functions of the teacher. A plant will not miss its end, nor will a newly hatched bird fail to fly. But without careful training a child will fail most tragically. Innate tendencies must be guided and controlled by the right kind of aims and motives if they are to strengthen rather than warp character. Their guidance and development is a part of the teacher's task.

5. *Not Totally Suppressed*

There is a persistence about these instinctive urges that is remarkable. If neglected they may wane, as in the case of the little chicken on the glass floor. But if the effort is made to suppress inner urges they will not down. If denied one channel of expression, they will in some way find another. Like the dammed up stream, they will make a way out through other channels. There is a persistence about drives that is astounding. We cannot get away either from their continuance or their effects. If one cannot preserve his life through honest labor, he will probably do it otherwise.

There are several of these outlets for inner drives. One is *imagination*. The bashful boy, too shy to get into society, may imagine himself a hero because of some deed done. The unattractive girl may see herself as the center of attraction because of scholarship. This is daydreaming, which may become a substitute for achievement. Sometimes an outlet is found through *separation*. If one's religious convictions will not allow him to engage in certain activities, he may simply think of the two as not related and do as he pleases. Sometimes people resort to *justification*. Many have drunk the whiskey they wanted while claiming the need for a stimulant for their tasks. This is a defense attitude and a risky one. It may be assumed without one's realizing its existence.

IV. SIGNIFICANCE OF URGES

We come now to consider the significance of instinctive drives for the teacher. Already this matter has been touched upon to some extent. However, we shall carry it further here, for after all this is the most important part of the topic. There are many ways in which instinctive urges have a bearing on character. We shall notice briefly a few of these ways. Other points may well be added.

1. *Awaken Interests*

The bursting forth of a new instinctive drive means the appearance of a new interest. Frequently this interest has a strong emotional element. For example, as the sex drive develops, the boy, instead of hating girls, is thrilled by them; and he pays much more attention to his clothes and general appearance. Previously he was interested in the gang. Likewise, when a religiously taught youngster reaches the age of accountability, he recognizes his aloofness from Christ, realizes his need of religion, and becomes interested in it. The same principle holds true for other drives.

This awakening of interests means that the teacher needs to be alert to developments and to take advantage of them. As William James once said: "In all pedagogy the great thing is to strike while the iron is hot, and to seize the wave of the pupil's interest in each successive subject before its ebb has come." [3] It is this development which determines the law of readiness. This means that when one is ready for an experience, to have it is enjoyable and to be denied it is annoying. The exact opposite is true when one is not ready. So the teacher must be on the alert for the appearance of new interests and capitalize on them. This principle of readiness is inherent in the use of activity teaching on the part of workers with little children.

2. *Stimulate Activities*

These urges or drives are not static but dynamic. They stir to action. Youngsters in a class are not passive but all steamed up and ready to go. The driving forces of human life are instinctive urges. Self-preservation spurs the lazy person to activity. The social urge causes even the most bashful to seek the companionship of others. Curiosity leads the reticent student to the most painstaking investigation. If the teacher desires a certain response, he can secure it by tying in with the appropriate drive. One can use the desire for approval of others to secure a better Sunday school lesson or a better discussion in a Training Union.

Instinctive drives are thus the handles on which the teacher can lay hold to get things done. It is partly for this reason that projects are so valuable, especially for Juniors and Intermediates. As William McDougall has said:

> Take away these instinctive dispositions with their powerful impulses and the organism would lie inert and motionless like a powerful clock whose mainspring had been removed or a steam engine whose fire had been drawn. These impulses are the mental forces that maintain and shape all the life of individuals and societies.[4]

3. *Become Storm Centers*

Because of their dynamic element, instinctive drives become the storm centers of life. The real battles of life are primarily within rather than without. These urges are the centers around which the most serious temptations arise. Passion can overcome the highest purpose and drag the finest person down. Miserliness can spoil a splendid life. The craving for power can lead to all sorts of evils. Pride can mar a beautiful soul. Even Paul fought to keep his body under, lest having preached to others he himself should become a castaway.

So pupils, as well as teachers, should be on the alert to get the upper hand of their inner urges. Many a juvenile delinquent could have been saved had he been guided aright. Much crime and immorality have grown out of the desire for social approval. The "gang" is the source of much trouble. Creative activities in Vacation Bible school, a good church recreational program, and an active Boy Scout troop or Royal Ambassador organization may be the means of saving many from the pitfalls of evil. The whole program of mental health is involved. Prevention is still better than cure.

4. *Develop into Character*

Just as instinctive drives awaken new interests and activities, so also do they lead to the development of habits and character. Particularly is this true if pleasurable results come from the expression of the drive. This fact is based on the idea that a satisfactory experience is likely to be repeated, and that the more often repeated the more sure it is to become a fixed habit. For example, the neglect of the social urge tends toward making a hermit, while its development leads to a congenial personality. Too much submissiveness destroys initiative, and too much self-assertion produces ultra-independence.

The significance of this principle is evident. What starts as a particular interest winds up as a permanent habit. Character is largely an accumulation or bundle of habits. It is largely made, for good or bad, through one's responses to instinctive urges. Life is thus crystallized around and shaped by the dominant interests and drives.

If money seems to satisfy one's urges adequately the individual comes to love money and to have faith in it. If a belief in God satisfies an instinctive desire for security, the individual develops a love for and faith in God. Happiness consists in finding an ever attainable group of satisfactions for all of the instinctive urges.[5]

5. *Need to Be Understood*

It is evident from what has been said that instincts must be properly evaluated. There have been two extreme views in this matter. One is the view that nature is right and instinctive desires should be given full freedom. It says that whatever is natural is beautiful and good. As to self-preservation, it endorses fighting and the survival of the fittest. It virtually encourages the idea of sowing wild oats. Some have said that by allowing free expression of instinctive desires one purges himself of them. Instead, he ingrains them and forms habits.

The opposite view is that instinctives desires are all wrong and must be crushed out. That was the feeling of the pious person who said that ice cream must be from the devil because it was so good. The Trappist monk goes to the extreme in retreating into a monastery, refusing to talk, refraining from meats, sleeping on boards, eating out of tin plates, rising at 2:00 A.M. for prayer, spending a while weekly before an open grave, and scourging his body daily. Human nature may be bad, but it is not that bad.

6. *Require the Proper Guidance*

Both of the views just discussed are extremes. Between them is the proper view, namely, instinctive urges must be handled and directed. Covetousness needs to be controlled. The same is true of extreme self-assertion. Even discipline may be necessary at times. But since all drives serve helpful purposes, they must be nurtured to a certain degree if a well-rounded personality is to result. As someone has suggested, it is better to say to a lively boy "Wiggle thus," than "Don't wiggle." It is better to take a boy on a hike than to turn him loose on the streets.

It is at this point of self-control that the matter of ideals comes in. A girl out with others refused to smoke cigarettes when all the others indulged and tried to get her to join. A young man refused free beer when all the others in the party participated. Proper ideals on amusements, honesty, purity, and greed will go a long way in holding inner urges in check. Proper motives serve as checks. The motives of fear, gain, and regard can be stressed as incentives to control inner drives. Inspiring examples from the Bible and history are very valuable. Thus can instinctive drives be woven into the fabric of character, and this is the end toward which we strive in all our teaching.

SUGGESTIONS FOR CLASS DISCUSSION

1. Which is the most powerful instinctive urge? Why?
2. What is meant by saying that instinctive drives are neither good nor bad?
3. What is the difference between an instinct and the emotional accompaniment?
4. What three characteristics are most important?
5. Mention values of instinctive urges other than those given.

[1] George B. Cutten, *Instincts and Religion* (New York: Harper and Bros., 1949), p. 8.

[2] Quoted by Grace Stuart, *The Achievement of Personality* (New York: The Macmillan Co., 1938), p. 26. Used by permission of publisher.

[3] William James, *The Principles of Psychology* (New York: Henry Holt and Co., Inc., 1918), II, 401.

[4] William McDougall, *Social Psychology* (Boston: Bruce Humphries, Inc., 1921), pp. 45–46.

[5] Ernest M. Ligon, *Psychology of Christian Personality* (New York: The Macmillan Co., 1935), p. 26. Used by permission of publisher.

CHAPTER 3

I. NATURE OF TEMPERAMENT

II. TYPES OF TEMPERAMENT
1. Physiological Approach
2. Psychological Approach

III. DETERMINANTS OF TEMPERAMENT
1. Race
2. Sex
3. Age
4. Glands
5. Other Influences

IV. RESULTS OF TEMPERAMENT
1. Persons Face Life Differently
2. Individuals Approach Christ Variously
3. Religious Experience Is Manifested Diversely
4. People Enjoy Varied Church Activities
5. Workers Are Fitted for Different Tasks

3

Temperamental Trends

ONE OF THE MOST NOTICEABLE facts about human life is the difference in people. Just as no two leaves in the forest are alike, so no two human beings are alike. Each is made according to a different pattern. These variations constitute a significant fact in human life. What the nature of these differences is, what causes them, how they affect life, and what should be done about them, we need to know. While a few books have dealt rather extensively with temperament, on the whole it has been largely neglected. If those who raise hogs or cattle need to know their differences, certainly religious teachers should be alert to the variations in pupils.

I. NATURE OF TEMPERAMENT

Some have used the word "temperament" as practically identical with the terms mood or disposition. Literally the word carries the idea of a mixture, suggesting the mixing or blending of the elements in one's bodily make-up. Years ago James H. Snowden characterized temperament as

> the emotional pitch to which one is keyed, the tonic note of all his music—the sounding board to all his moods, an emotional lens that gives character and color to all his experiences. All his mental states sift through his temperament, as light through a stained glass window, and are tinged by its hues.[1]

In general, the term is used to describe a person's characteristic state or mood. It is, therefore, the tone or pitch of life. Practically, we think of temperament as that which determines the way we look at or respond to life. For example, two persons with the same parents and brought up in the same home, will be interested in very different things. The variations in people are largely the result of temperament. It is the source of many of the striking differences between individuals, and it determines much of the outlook on life, cast of thought, and line of action.

It is evident from the foregoing statements that temperament influences very much one's view of, and attitude toward, life. It determines largely the characteristic emotional tone of an individual's personality. It is a pervasive influence affecting the quality of one's behavior, including mood, alertness, and speed of action. Temperament has much to do with attitudes and conduct. It is not something incidental in life; it is at the heart of personality differences.

II. TYPES OF TEMPERAMENT

The classification of temperament varies according to the viewpoint taken. Some approach it from the physical point of view and seek a biological basis for it. Others take the psychological approach and classify on that basis. People cannot be arbitrarily placed into groups. Rather they are dominantly of one type or another.

1. *Physiological Approach*

The oldest and most commonly used classifications of temperamental types come to us from Greek history. They had four groups, based on four supposed "humors" in the body: blood, bile, black bile, and phlegm. While inadequate as to the causes, the Greeks were rather good in description— though of course one could not divide a congregation into the four groups; there is overlapping and duplication.

One type is the *sanguine*. The word means "blood" and suggests an abundance of it. The sanguine people are warmhearted, enthusiastic, vivacious, and great people to preach to. Evangelists and promoters belong generally to this group, as do many book agents. Billy Bray, the famous Cornish preacher, demonstrated this type when he said: "If they were to put me into a barrel I would shout glory out through the bunghole." Saint Catherine, Cardinal Newman, and John Wesley are also said to have belonged to the sanguine group. This type is fitted to lead a needy cause.

> It is the sanguine who please and persuade other people into geniality. Their infectious personalities have unseen antennae that reach out and stimulate our affection. The Christianized sanguine temperament is a great temperament for a death bed.[2]

However sanguine people may be too spontaneous, over-enthusiastic, blind to consequences, and lacking in stability. Probably unfairly, they have been characterized as the "quick-weak" type.

Another type is the *choleric*. The term refers to bile, which was thought to contribute to anger. This type is energetic, dynamic, and aggressive. It is characterized by impatience. Moses impulsively killed an Egyptian, and struck the rock instead of speaking to it. John was very appropriately called "son of thunder." Carlyle was said to have "a daily secretion of curses he was bound to vent on some one." The choleric temperament helps to furnish the holy anger needed to put a good cause through. This type is steady and persistent and furnishes generals for armies, administrators for business, and executives for government. It may become too domineering. It is the "quick-strong" type. Stevenson says:

> No committee is complete without one specimen of the choleric temperament——. Further no committee ought to harbor more than one specimen of the temperament. While the melancholic are . . . anticipating deficits, the phlegmatic pondering amendments, and the sanguine prophesying, the choleric will . . . hustle the good cause to show of success.[3]

The *melancholic* is the third type. The word literally means "black bile." This type is liable to be dreary, sad, and brooding. In fact, he may become morbid and pessimistic. Elijah under the juniper tree wishing he might die, Jeremiah proclaiming his sad messages, and Hosea with his anguish of spirit, are examples of the melancholic temperament. The Puritan is said to be the typical example. Such people make great mystics, reveal the inward strength of religion, but have to be on their guard against morbid fatalism. This temperament furnishes many of our artists, poets, and musicians. Like Spanish music, they may weave a minor note into their chords. This has been designated as the "slow-strong" type.

> Have not the melancholy furnished Paul among apostles, Livingstone among missionaries, Dante among poets, Cromwell among statesmen—, Bunyan among dreamers, Savonarola among reformers and Michelangelo among painters? [4]

The last of these types is the *phlegmatic*. The word suggests an abundance of "phlegm" and indicates that there is something within the person that clogs his movements. Persons of this type are slow, calm, patient, and matter-of-fact. They plod along, keeping the even tenor of their way. They love routine, are lacking in initiative, and need prodding.

> Their main difficulty is ignition—. They rarely come out of the garage on their own power. But once they really take the road they may be depended on for a lengthy run. [5]

They are not too progressive but are very dependable. They are masters of the art of playing second fiddle. They follow routine, regularity, and habit. The Chinese coolie is a typical example. Phlegmatic persons fill necessary and helpful places in society and furnish the ballast for the ship of state. Queen Anne, King Albert, and Herbert Spencer are said to have belonged to this type. It has been called the "slow-weak" type.

2. *Psychological Approach*

In modern times there has been a very different classification of temperament. It has much of its origin in Germany and is definitely psychological in its point of view.

First is the *introvert*. The word literally means "to turn in," and suggests the tendency to turn one's thoughts in upon himself and to introspect his own inner, mental processes. This type is rather mystical and self-centered in its emphasis. The person enjoys solitary worship.

> He is intensely subjective in his thoughts and emotions. He is shy and inhibited, does not adjust readily to new social situations. He shrinks when met by a crisis, is easily hurt, slow in making decisions, uncomfortable when in the focus of social attention, given to imagination rather than action, turns to introspection, is meticulous in the care of his person.[6]

This is the type suitable for life in a monastery or convent. The danger is that they may brood over their problems, worry too much, and flee from reality.

Over against the foregoing type is the *extrovert*. Instead of his thoughts and interests being turned upon himself, the extrovert's interests are turned outward toward others. He thinks more in terms of people and external affairs than of philosophies. He is objective and is a good salesman, politician, or social leader. Such people are practical and become absorbed in service. "Others" is their motto. As the introvert is inclined to flee from reality, so the extrovert flees into reality and is relatively free from mental difficulties. It was this value of losing oneself in service to others that led Henry C. Link to put extroversion at the very heart of personality development and mental health.

The third psychological type is the *ambivert*. As the word indicates, this type is a combination of introvert and extrovert, or it may be one who shifts from one to the other. The Old Testament prophet was often both mystical and practical in nature. This is something of the ideal type, since it has the quality of both and is, therefore, more balanced and well-rounded. It suggests the goal we should seek.

Norman E. Richardson once emphasized the theological aspect of temperament. The *traditionalist* versus the *critical* means one who reverences the past and keeps things as they are, over against one who practices evaluation and improvement. The *mystical* versus the *executive* suggests those who stress feelings and values, over against those who deal in programs and activities. The *ritualist* versus the *propagandist* pictures the one who likes the formal and ceremonial, in contrast to one who likes campaigns and promotion. And the *ascetic* versus the *reformer* describes the person who stresses self-denial and mortifying the flesh, over against the one who works for social changes and improvements.

Each of these various types has its elements of strength as well as weakness. Each needs something of the other, and it takes all kinds to give completeness to a social group. It would be rather unfortunate for society if all people were of the same type of temperament. Ideally, it would be fine if each individual could have some of the strong points of all of the temperaments. Within limits, development may be made in this direction.

III. DETERMINANTS OF TEMPERAMENT

Several factors enter into the shaping of temperament. Each plays its part. How far each affects temperament, we can hardly say. All to some extent have an influence.

1. *Race*

Race has much to do with temperament. The Negro is characteristically carefree and optimistic, worrying very little. The Spanish people weave a minor note into their music, indicating an element of sadness. The English are rather stolid and unemotional, but hold tenaciously the ground gained. French people are enthusiastic and vivacious, as was witnessed when Lindberg landed in Paris. People in India have, in the past, been generally rather submissive and nonprogressive. The Chinese are plodders, carrying with a merry pace their heavy loads in baskets on a pole on their shoulders. Some students of psychology have even sought to classify nations according to temperament, saying the French are sanguine, the Germans choleric, the Spanish melancholic, and the English phlegmatic. This classification is suggestive but not absolutely accurate. Environment and culture must also be considered in studying temperament.

2. Sex

Some of the most noticeable temperamental differences are between men and women. These differences are never quite overcome, even when the two sexes are brought up in the same home, go through the same school, and engage in the same occupation. Men and women are different constitutionally, with different attitudes, interests, and customs. Most men cannot take the interests in hats and hairdos that women do. Nor are women likely to be as much interested in politics and stock markets as men are, even though the women wear pants and work in factories. However much a father bereft of his wife tries to take her place in the life of his children, he can never fully succeed. Neither can the mother entirely take the father's place in the world of business and statecraft. Men and women are different, and no amount of wishing can change this fact.

3. Age

Differences in age, with their accompanying physiological and psychological changes, bring personality variations. An individual is not the same at various stages in life. The quiet infant, eating, and sleeping in the crib shows few of the traits he will have later. The trustful, playful child is very different from the same person in later adolescence. The turbulent early adolescent is much unlike the more settled person of middle life. And the enthusiastic college student is very different in later years. Adulthood brings a more settled and mature attitude. Someone has said that the sanguine temperament characterizes childhood, the melancholic youth, the choleric maturity, and the phlegmatic old age. This classification is not absolutely correct, but is an interesting suggestion. Each stage of maturation makes its contributions, and it takes all to make life complete. Each is complementary to the others, and life would be monotonous without all ages.

4. *Glands*

A very influential factor in temperament is glandular activity. The endocrine or ductless glands secrete their hormones directly into the blood stream and have a tremendous influence on the personality. One writer went so far as to suggest that glands regulate personality. This is of course carrying it a bit too far, but is suggestive.

> The happy guess that temperament, the emotional ground-work of personality, is conditioned above all else by body chemistry has been increasingly borne out in modern research.[7]

Others verify this idea. So it is well established that the underlying emotional tone of the individual is affected by the endocrine glands, as well as by other physical conditions.

The *pituitary* gland is located near the base of the brain. It secretes a hormone called tethelin, which is essential to growth. An undersupply of this hormone results in the dwarf or midget. An oversupply produces the giant.

The *thyroid* is located at the front of the throat near the pharynx. It secretes thyroxin, which has to do with the speed of living. An undersupply slows down activity and tends toward lethargy and sluggishness. An oversupply speeds up the bodily processes, causing excitability and nervousness.

The *adrenal* glands are located at the top of the kidneys. They have been called "the glands of combat." They supply adrenalin, which helps to meet emergencies. It has been said that the amount of adrenalin secretion in the blood makes the difference between the hero and the coward.

The *gonads* are located in the lower abdomen. They are the

sex glands and determine reproduction. They affect the development of the individual physically, mentally, and morally. Without their proper functioning, neither sex develops according to pattern.

Other glands include the *parathyroids,* supplying calcium. A deficiency in their supply results in nervousness, over-excitability, and muscular disorder. An oversupply brings about lethargy, lassitude, and lack of interest.

The *pancreatic* glands supply insulin, which regulates the supply of sugar to the body. A deficiency of this hormone brings diabetes. The result is thirst, hunger, and mental sluggishness.

Other glands include the *pineal,* which has to do with brightness or dumbness, and the *thymus,* which serves as a brake or check on other glandular activities, particularly sex. All of these are important and have a marked part to play in the development of personality. Malfunctioning of any one of these glands results in a disturbance of the organism.

5. *Other Influences*

Health affects temperament. The person of robust health radiates inspiration and encouragement. The one with poor health does just the opposite. The individual who is dyspeptic or bilious will be pessimistic and a poor leader. He is comparable to the salesman who knocked on a door and when the lady opened it said, "I guess you do not want to buy anything today, do you?" People with indigestion headaches do not inspire others.

Climate influences personality. The individual in the Frigid Zone spends much of his strength battling the elements and cannot be the genial person he otherwise would be. The person in the Torrid Zone is beaten down by the heat and does not have the energy to accomplish much. Those in a constantly rainy climate are not likely to be as optimistic and inspirational as those in a sunshiny atmosphere.

Environment has its bearing. This fact, of course, is involved in part in what has just been said. The man who spends his life in the secluded mountains will be rather different from the one who lives in the wide, open plains. The one who resides in the city is not quite like his country cousin. The slum-dweller is noticeably different from the person in a good residential area. We are inevitably affected by our environment.

Occupation leaves its stamp. The farmer is different from the businessman, the teacher from the lawyer, and the doctor from the salesman. Occupation so impresses itself on the individual that a keen psychologist can tell a man's occupation from his appearance. Outlook and attitude are both affected. The "ministerial voice" is usually recognizable. And one is not easily fooled by the back-slapping politician.

IV. RESULTS OF TEMPERAMENT

What bearing does temperament have on the life of the individual and on the work of the religious leader? There are several very interesting and significant things to be noted:

1. *Persons Face Life Differently*

Some people are naturally optimistic, the proverbial "sky-blue" characters. They look on the bright side of life, are eternally hopeful, and often trust others too much. While having their eyes on the stars, they need also to keep their feet on the ground. Others are just the opposite and are regularly pessimistic. They look on the dark side of things and see the obstacles rather than the opportunities. They pour cold water on new projects and spread their gloom to others. They need to be kept out of places of leadership.

There are those who are always dreaming. They have some utopia before them regularly. Their heads are always in the clouds. They are strong on faith and new ventures. They plan great things but never carry through. They need to be led to face realities. Others are very practical minded and scorn new ventures. They want to count the cost minutely and follow the beaten path. They need to be prodded. Each temperament needs the point of view of the others, and it takes all to complete life.

2. Individuals Approach Christ Variously

Psychologically, people are not alike in the way they approach Christ. They are drawn along different routes and through varied appeals. As George Steven has said:

> One is practical and builds up his faith on the Sermon on the Mount, and loves Christ as the great Social Leader; another is speculative and gets at his Lord through far-reaching ideas; while still another is mystical, believing he enters into the most personal communion with God, spirit to spirit.[8]

Whatever the avenue of approach all must come into a personal relation and vital union with Christ. Some will be appealed to largely through the intellect, while others will be reached mainly through the emotions. With some the vicarious death of Christ will make the strongest appeal, and with others it will be his matchless life. One will come mainly through the conviction of sin and the desire to get away from a bad past, while another will be drawn more through a conviction of righteousness and the desire to enter the larger life. Christ used both fear and love as appeals. Paul became "all things to all men." Different types of preachers will appeal to different people.

3. Religious Experience Is Manifested Diversely

People do not manifest their religious experience alike. With one individual, shouting is the natural and almost inevitable expression of conversion experience. Another will never shout, but will express his feeling through crying. A third will do neither of these, but will simply have a quiet smile. And a fourth will experience conversion, or any other deliberate decision, with no particular emotional manifestation. Paul and Matthew did not have the same experience.

All of this adds up to the fact that we cannot judge the value of religious experience by the way in which it is expressed. Those who show little or no emotion may have just as valuable an experience as those who shout or cry. It is the heart of the experience that counts. One consistant Christian in testifying during a revival said, "Brethren and sisters, I am just about normal." And normal with him meant a high plane of Christian living. It is the quality of life that counts.

4. People Enjoy Varied Church Activities

The same aspect of church life does not appeal to all people alike. Some will be drawn to a church because of the splendid music, beautiful architecture, processionals, and ritual. Others are attracted by a sensational or militant emphasis. Baptists and Episcopalians enjoy very different types of church services. It could almost be said that there is a psychological, as well as a theological, basis for various denominations. This fact may not justify them but it does help to explain them.

This means that churches should make their programs as rich and varied as possible so as to appeal to the interests of all types of people. Architecture, ritual, music, teaching, and preaching—all have their place. One writer has even suggested that one reason for more women than men in the average church service is that the program is more adapted to the feminine nature. This statement may be a bit extreme, but it does suggest the wisdom of taking into consideration different types of personalities.

5. Workers Are Fitted for Different Tasks

Not all people will perform the same task in a church equally well. Their backgrounds, interests, and activities fit them for varied phases of service. Some like administrative work and will do their best in an executive position. Others like teaching and will render their best ministry here, even with a particular age group. Still others are statistically inclined and will serve best in some secretarial position, as did an expert accountant the writer knew. Some are musicians and others are social leaders. God can regenerate any type of temperament and utilize it in the work of his kingdom.

All of this means that the leadership of the church should know the inclinations and interest of the different members and seek to fit each to the type of work he is most interested in. In other words, in church life as elsewhere we should avoid trying to fit "round pegs into square holes." Just as the eye, the ear, the hand, and other organs of the body have their distinctive services to perform, so it is in kingdom service, as Paul pointed out. Some are apostles, some prophets, and some teachers (1 Cor. 12:28).

SUGGESTIONS FOR CLASS DISCUSSION

1. Formulate a definition of temperament.
2. Appraise Dr. Richardson's approach to temperamental types.
3. Which of the determinants discussed do you think is strongest?
4. What other results of or values in temperament can you mention?

---

[1] James H. Snowden, *The Psychology of Religion* (Westwood, New Jersey: Fleming H. Revell Co., 1916), p. 42.

[2] J. C. Stevenson, *Religion and Temperament* (New York: Funk and Wagnalls Co.), p. 106.

[3] *Ibid.*, p. 151.

[4] *Ibid.*, p. 178.

[5] *Ibid.*, p. 67.

[6] George Herbert Betts, *Foundations of Character and Personality* (New York: The Bobbs-Merrill Co., Inc., 1937), p. 44. Used by permission of publisher.

[7] Gordon W. Allport, *Personality—A Psychological Interpretation* (New York: Henry Holt and Co., 1937), p. 64.

[8] George Steven, *The Psychology of the Christian Soul* (London: Hodder and Stoughton, Ltd., 1911), p. 184.

CHAPTER 4

I. THOUGHT
1. Perception
2. Memory
3. Imagination
4. Reason

II. FEELING
1. Kinds of Feeling
2. Importance of Feeling
3. Utilizing the Feelings

III. WILL
1. Types of Will
2. Phases of Will
3. Dealing with Will

4

Mental Activities

It is through the mind that a person reacts to heredity, environment, and experience, and it is these reactions which largely determine character. In this chapter we shall take a brief look at the various activities of the mind. An old but very valuable approach is to consider the intellectual, the emotional, and the volitional phases—or thought, feeling, and will. These aspects, to be sure, are not absolutely separate and distinct. Rather they overlap and interfuse; there is some of all in each. There is some feeling in all thinking and some action in both. But this division does give a very helpful approach in studying the various aspects of mental life.

I. Thought

The thinking phase of mental life has to do with intellectual processes or the acquiring of knowledge. It is the process by which the person comes to understand himself, the world in which he lives, and those around him. There are several aspects of thinking.

1. *Perception*

The word itself carries the *meaning* of "taking in." As Henry E. Garrett says: "Perception is that organizing process by which we come to know objects in their appropriate identity as trees, men, buildings, machines, and so on." [1] Perception involves interpreting the raw materials given by sensations. It is the mind's response to the impressions that come through the senses. It is somewhat like the picture produced on the photographer's negative. It provides us with factual materials for our mental life, or the grist for the mill of thought. Effective thinking requires accurate perception.

There are two *aspects* of the process of perception. One is the receiving of sensations through the five senses: sight, sound, touch, taste, and smell. This is somewhat like the calls that come over the wires to the telephone operator. The other aspect is the interpretation of these sensations. For example, impressions of something red, round, and about the size of a ball come in through the senses and are interpreted as an apple. Proper interpretation depends on the accuracy of the sensations and on past experience. A fern is a "green feather" and an alligator a "big lizard" to a little child because of his limited experience. The botanist and the hired hand get very different meanings from the rose. This is back of J. M. Gregory's law of teaching: "The truth to be taught must be learned through truth already known."

There are several *aids* in perceiving. One is the use of maps, charts, chalkboards, pictures, and objects. Since probably three fourths of what we learn comes through the eye, much of the material from which we form percepts will be received through visual means. For the blind person, of course, hearing and touch are the most effective channels. Another aid to perception is the story. The imagination helps one to see the things pictured in the story. The dramatic method is also valuable, since there is the acting out of the scene, adding movement to the visual. Herein is much of the power of the picture show and television. Association of events and places likewise helps in perceiving. For example, Paul's journeys will be much better understood by tying the history and the geography together as we study.

2. *Memory*

As to its *nature*, memory is the process by which we retain in our minds the percepts acquired. It is a sort of storehouse for ideas, and also a workshop, changing to some extent the impressions that come in. There are four steps in a complete process of memory: reception of the percept into the mind, retention of it, reproduction or bringing it back to the focus of attention, and recognition or identifying it. It is evident that but for memory we would have to learn everything all over again each day. "Life is rich," said Goethe, "as we fill it with things beautiful to remember." Much of the pangs of hell and the joys of heaven are wrapped up in memories.

There are at least three *kinds* of memory. One is verbal, in which the very words are recalled. This type is characteristic of childhood, reaching its height about the Junior period. So later childhood is a fine time to store up choice biblical passages and doctrinal truths of importance to the child. Catholics have used this principle effectively in teaching the catechism.

Another kind of memory is associative. In this case a thing is remembered because of its connection with something else either in space or time. For instance, it helps to fix both facts in mind if one notes that Abraham Lincoln and Jefferson Davis were born in adjoining counties a year apart. One may compare Elijah and John the Baptist profitably, or contrast Judas and Paul to advantage.

Thought memory is the third kind. Here we recall not the words but the substance of the statement. The idea is kept in mind. This kind of memory is characteristic of young people and adults.

There are several *helps* in remembering. One is recency. The more recent a thing is, the more readily it is recalled. One can recall much more of a lesson immediately after it is taught than he will if he waits a week. Reviews, therefore, are very important.

Frequency is another help in remembering. The more often a thing is repeated the more likely it is to be remembered. This is the reason the chorus of a song is remembered best.

Frequent use of Scripture passages helps to fix them in the memory.

Intensity is a third aid to memory. The more vivid and impressive a thing is, the more likely it is to be remembered. One will remember a serious automobile wreck that he sees better than he will one he merely hears about. Teaching therefore should have an element of feeling and conviction and should utilize as many avenues of perception as possible.

3. *Imagination*

A good *definition* of imagination would be that it is the picture-making or image-forming function of the mind. By means of this activity the individual brings before his mind images of people, places, and events far removed in time and space. He may transport himself to the ends of the earth and imagine travel experiences. The imagination gives substance to things not seen and is, therefore, closely akin to faith. It covers the ground of memory and goes beyond into things which have not been experienced. It has been characterized as "the eye of the soul." Through the imagination we see the unseen and make real that which is not present.

In general there are three *types* of imagination. One is the reproductive, by which the mind brings before itself past scenes and experiences. In this respect it has much in common with memory. The reverie of the elderly person is very largely of this kind.

Another type is the interpretative, by which the individual makes real scenes and events that he has not experienced. By studying the facts, he can put himself imaginatively into the situation being studied and see it more clearly. A vivid imagination of this type is very helpful in interpreting the Scriptures.

Creative imagination is the third type. It takes scenes and events with which we are not familiar and makes them real. New combinations are worked out from things that are familiar. Inventions, poems, paintings, and songs are the result of the creative imagination.

There are distinct *values* in imagination. By it the understanding is clarified. One cannot understand the Bible properly unless he can put himself imaginatively into the situation described and see it through the eyes of those who participated. For example, we can better appreciate John's statement regarding heaven when he said, "The sea is no more" (Rev. 21:1 ASV), if we can picture his situation as an exile on an island. Through the imagination we can sympathize with someone in distress as we put ourselves in his place. This projection into another's place is greatly needed as we deal with the poor, the suffering, the aged, and the bereaved. We would do more for the benighted and starving millions around the world if we realized more clearly their condition. Likewise, ideals are shaped through the imagination. Washington organized his playmates into an army and drilled them. During his trips into the South, Lincoln visualized freeing the slaves. Through the imagination we make real the unseen.

4. *Reason*

As to its *nature*, reason is that activity of mind by which we take the materials furnished us through perception and combine them into new wholes. It is the weighing and evaluating activity of the mind. By it we compare, contrast, classify, and work over ideas and form conclusions. We gather all of the facts possible and form general principles. Reason is one of the most important phases of human life, lifting the individual above the animal and the unthinking. It contributes to dominion over the forces of nature, animal life, and all creation. Science, invention, and progress grow out of it.

There are several *hindrances* to correct thinking. Prejudice and desire may interfere. A person may be so prejudiced against a thing as to be unable to see the facts regarding it. Or, his desire may be so strong that he cannot consider the other side of the issue. The wish is often father to the thought. Dependence on tradition and the opinion of others may also prevent thinking a thing through. Many ideas about the Bible come through unquestioned acceptance of tradition. Also, lack of observation and experience may handicap a person in seeing a thing in its true light. So we have to be on guard in our thinking.

Likewise there are a number of *aids* to right thinking. One is an open mind to receive the truth, from whatever source it comes. This is much easier said than done, but it is very important. A prominent preacher once said that he welcomed criticism from anyone; it helped him to evaluate himself. Another important aid to good thinking is getting all of the facts. Judgment should always be reserved until all of the facts are in. Getting facts takes time and effort. Teachers should stimulate students at this point.

II. FEELING

Along with thought is the matter of feeling. In fact the two intermingle. There is an element of feeling in all thinking, and vice versa. One is influenced by his emotions quite as much as by his thoughts. Often inner feelings color thinking. Most of life's problems are approached heart foremost. We always do the thing we actually want most to do.

1. Kinds of Feeling

The first and lowest level of feeling is *sensation*. By this is meant the pleasant or unpleasant tone that accompanies all activity. It is the agreeable or disagreeable feeling growing out of bodily conditions, environmental influences, or life experiences. It is closely related to the physical and involves pleasure or pain. Indigestion can make one very unhappy. Bad health may result in a pessimistic disposition, which may in turn crystallize into a permanent mood. Physical punishment is not the highest level of discipline, but it has its place, since it involves sensation. A child learns to avoid whatever is unpleasant. Life and character are definitely affected by the feeling tone from day to day.

Emotion constitutes another aspect of the feeling life. As the word indicates, it is rather intense. An emotion is often rather stormy, rises suddenly, and often produces physical effects. Grief finds expression in tears, amusement in laughter, and happiness in smiles. Emotion includes such states as anger, fear, hate, love, grief, and joy. These are the accompaniments of instinctive tendencies—anger leading to fighting, fear to running away, grief to tears, and love to service. Egotistic emotions center in self, resulting in pride, egoism, and the desire for approval. They may be utilized for good through the employment of grades, awards, and approval. Altruistic emotions center in others and include such states as friendship, sympathy, and love. They determine one's attitudes toward the widow, the orphan, and the down-and-out. Emotions are the drive behind actions and are close to the heart of character.

Sentiments are the highest kind of feeling. A sentiment is an organized system of emotions centered about some object. Just as emotions are more complex than sensations, so sentiments are more complex than emotions and a bit more abstract. Reverence, loyalty, and patriotism are examples of sentiments, as are pride, jealousy, and revenge. Character is to a great extent the crystallization of sentiments. Nothing is more sublime than loyalty to a great cause, nor more debasing than revenge gone wrong. Heroes and martyrs are made of people dominated by sublime sentiments. Charles W. Elliott once said: "The world is still governed by sentiments. National greatness and righteousness depend more on the cultivation of right sentiments in children than anything else."

2. *Importance of Feeling*

The way one feels largely *determines worth*. Our sense of worth grows out of the affective consciousness more than it does out of the intellect. Our judgments of relative values are rooted in the sentiments. How we feel toward a thing is more significant than what we think about it. Nothing is of great value to the person with a bursting headache. Atheists are made such more by the heart than by the head. The gilded saloon and jovial company have much to do with the inclination to drink. One will purchase things under the sway of music at a sale that otherwise he would not buy. The Sunday school teacher who is liked will be more effective than one who is disliked, even though the latter is brilliant. William James once said, "Our judgments concerning the worth of things big or little depend on the feelings the things arouse in us."

As already intimated, *activities are influenced* by the emotions. What we do depends largely on the way we feel. James H. Snowden says:

> The feelings pour their flood upon the will as a stream upon a wheel, or as steam into the cylinder upon the piston that drives the engine—or as a spark that explodes the powder.[2]

A father will steal before he will see his family suffer. A mother, worn threadbare by the toils of the day, can sit up all night by the crib of a sick child. A little girl, when asked if the big baby she was carrying up the hill was not too heavy, replied, "No, he is my brother." Disappointment in love or ambition may spur one on to greater achievements—or paralyze his activities. A parent can lift off a hurt child a load that otherwise he could not handle.

Happiness is affected. It has been said that whether or not life is worth living depends "on the conditions of the liver." How true this is! The state of one's health may determine whether or not he wants to go on living. Suicides are often the result of depression. The person consumed by pride is an unhappy individual. The same is true with one dominated by jealousy, hatred, or fear. The spoiled child is anything but happy. The melancholic individual is pitiful. On the other hand, sympathy, love, and joy make for a happy individual. As one is dominated by wholesome emotions, life is made worthwhile. "Out of it [the heart] are the issues of life" (Prov. 4:23).

3. Utilizing the Feelings

How shall we utilize the feelings in developing Christian character? For one thing, we should seek to *restrain wrong emotions*. Anger, if carried too far, may lead to an uncontrollable temper. Fear may develop a cowardly type of person. Lust can bring about the most degraded life. Self-depreciation may lead to a sense of inferiority; pride can carry to the opposite extreme. The individual should be led to stay away from situations that stimulate undesirable attitudes. Such stimulation may result from harmful picture shows, dance halls, and drinking places. It may also come from certain types of books and comics that incline toward crime, immorality, and other evils. Good young people have been led into crime by bad literature and shows. Similarly, innocent youngsters have been tempted into immorality. "Shun the very appearance of evil" is good advice.

Over against restraining wrong emotions is the need to *stimulate right affections*. "Overcome evil with good" is a fine motto. Paul says: "Set your affection on things above" (Col. 3:2). Love should be developed for things that are right, such as purity, honesty, and truthfulness. Reverence for the Bible, the church, the sabbath, and moral standards should be cultivated. After a group of high school boys had tied a can to a cat's tail and scared it nearly to death, the principal got them to adopt the cat as the mascot of their ball team. Then they cared for it tenderly instead of abusing it. Sympathy for the poor, help for the needy, concern for peoples without the gospel may be developed. Stories, pictures, and music will help. Biographical illustrations and reading are very valuable.

Care should be taken *not to overstimulate the emotions.* It is possible to go too far in the matter of arousing emotions, and a rebound will follow. Some people spend too much time reading sentimental literature, attending emotional plays, and even going to church to have their feelings stirred up. They become "emotional addicts." To them a service is not spiritual unless it makes them cry. Herein is the danger of highly wrought worship programs, revival meetings, and consecration services. They "fire up the engine to watch the wheels go around." As a result many individuals fall down on their professions of faith, commitments for life service, and financial pledges, and their last state is often worse than the first. When emotions are stimulated, opportunities for action should be provided or the person may be harmed. We are as responsible for the souls whose experiences we bungle as we are for those we fail to reach.

III. WILL

The third aspect of mental life is the will, or the volitional activity. The following statements show its significance:

> It keeps the intellect at work, or lets it idle; it keeps unseemly emotions in subjection, or lets them overwhelm us; it realizes the capacity which heredity bestows, or wraps it in a napkin; it improves the opportunity which environment allows or fatally neglects it; it stems the current of adverse circumstances, or drifts indifferently into an alien port.[3]

> A dominant will pushes a railroad over the plains; spans the surging stream with a suspension bridge; overcomes a malignant pestilence; proposes a league of nations; expounds and champions a new religion.[4]

Without will there would be no action and so no habit or achievement.

1. *Types of Will*

One type is the *deliberative.* That is the kind of will the foregoing quotations picture. It grows more out of thought than of impulse. It is the result of conscious deliberation. One considers all of the consequences of an act and then makes up his mind. He awakens on a cold, rainy Sunday and has to decide whether or not to go to church. He faces a life choice, weighs all of the consequences, and makes his decision. The future as well as the present is taken into consideration. Alternatives are carefully evaluated. All angles of the case are considered. Most of the significant events of life are faced in this fashion. Deliberative will is will at its highest, and definitely marks off man from the lower orders of life.

But there is another type of will that is just as real, though we do not always consider it so. This is the *spontaneous* type. In this case a decision is made without due deliberation, as when Moses struck the rock and when Peter made his rash pledge. One sees an open door and rises to close it, perceives an apple and reaches for it, hears the church bell and starts to Sunday school. Eating, dressing, and many other activities are after this fashion. "I did it before I thought," is a common statement. Interest, desire, and habit have much to do with the spontaneous deed. It is simply the expression of our normal selves. The wish is father to the act. Sometimes there are needed the cautions: "Look before you leap," and "Think twice before you speak."

2. *Phases of Will*

The first stage in an act of deliberative will is *weighing* the consequences. With two or more alternatives before one, there is the necessity of deciding which is the better course. Confronted with a forked-road situation, one must decide which way to go. If the deliberation is about a college education, a person must consider the time, money, and energy.

A young woman may face the question of marriage before finishing college. A young person may consider the matter of going to a foreign mission field. With an open mind and adequate information, he weighs all of the evidence and comes to a conclusion. The teacher should help people think through vital problems.

After having considered the alternatives pro and con, the individual must at last arrive at a *decision*. This is the crux of the whole matter. Otherwise he is like the individual shivering on the bank of the pool unable to make up his mind to jump in. There must be a choice if anything is done. An unselfish attitude is essential. A good environment will be of value. Previous decision also will help, and proper motives are important. The Sunday school teacher will help to develop motives and guide the pupil over the hill. Making the decision is the crisis point in an act of will.

3. *Dealing with Will*

For one thing we should *realize the place* of will in character building. There can be no strength of character without it, for character is made up largely of habits that are determined by acts of will. In a sense, it is the sum total of the acts of will. John Stuart Mill has said: "Character is nothing more than a perfectly-fashioned will." Life is significant as it issues in acts and habits. A person devoid of will power will always be a weakling—helpless and spineless. This fact is seen particularly in those who take narcotics. Hence, developing the will is at the heart of character building.

Also we should allow persons to *exercise their own wills*. The parent who chooses all the changes for a child does him irretrievable harm. He will learn to depend on the parent— as did the girl who enrolled in a seminary, got her textbooks, attended classes, and at the end of the first week went back home with her mother. She was tied to her mother's apron strings. This situation frequently causes trouble with young wives who do not know how to make a decision without mother's help. It is seen also in a dictatorship. A poor democracy is better than a good monarchy. A person must be led to make his own decisions.

But individuals should not be left entirely alone. Teachers should *stimulate proper decisions*. One learns self-direction by being given encouragement to make his own choices. We must not stop with merely telling pupils what is right; we must help them to make decisions. This is done by stimulating suggestions. Also, good illustrations will help. We may well work on the individual's motives in helping to get action. The impulsive power of a new affection is good. Moses looked for the "recompense of the reward" and Christ for "the joy that was set before him." Self gain and social approval are desirable, but obligation to God is a higher motive.

SUGGESTIONS FOR CLASS DISCUSSION

1. What is the relation of memory to the subconsciousness?
2. Illustrate the power of the imagination.
3. Show the value of reason.
4. What is the difference between emotion and sentiment?
5. How is the will best influenced?

[1] Henry E. Garrett, *Psychology* (New York: American Book Co., 1955), p. 155. Used by permission.

[2] James H. Snowden, *The Psychology of Religion* (Westwood, N. J.: Fleming H. Revell Co., 1916), p. 46.

[3] H. H. Horne, *Psychological Principles of Education* (New York: The Macmillan Co., 1912), pp. 261–262. Used by permission of publisher.

[4] W. S. Athearn, *An Introduction to the Study of the Mind* (Philadelphia: The Westminster Press, 1912), p. 163.

CHAPTER 5

I. THE HOME
   1. Advantages
   2. Handicaps
   3. Tasks

II. THE CHURCH
   1. Importance
   2. Organizations
   3. Achievements

III. THE SCHOOL
   1. Opportunities
   2. Weaknesses
   3. Accomplishments

5

Social Agencies

IN THE PRECEDING CHAPTERS we have dealt mainly with factors inherent in the individual. These, as we have seen, furnish the potentialities of Christian character, or the raw material out of which it is made. Now we turn to the environmental forces that play upon the individual and his reactions to them. These also definitely enter into the formation of character. Margaret Slattery, speaking of a little infant, said:

> She was so perfectly helpless—the world could make anything out of her. Her parents would teach her any language they chose—. At school she would learn what state and city had determined. She would seek God by the Methodist—Baptist—Catholic—Hebrew pathway, according to the church to which her parents led her.[1]

Of course we must not discount the power of God to overcome human influences, but there is much truth in Miss Slattery's comment. Social agencies do count. Parents and teachers need to understand these influences so as to work with the child to the best advantage. The Catholics furnish a striking example of what a denomination can do to shape the religious life of the child.

I. THE HOME

The first agency influencing the child is the home. In many respects it is the most influential and, therefore, bears a large part of the burden. Yet not all of the responsibility for the child's outcome can be placed upon the home, since other agencies of society play their part.

1. *Advantages*

For one thing the home has the child *first*. Before other agencies have a chance, the home gets in its influence. From almost the beginning, as the little one lies helplessly on its back in its crib, it is drinking in the expressions and attitudes of those who wait on it. This fact is most significant, for first impressions are likely to be the most influential and lasting. Also the beginning period of life is the time when the child is most impressionable. Never again will he be so easily influenced by external forces. In childhood, curiosity is strongest, feelings are tenderest, and lifetime habits are being formed. The child is indeed like a piece of plastic clay in the hands of the potter. And, too, childhood is the time of greatest external control. Soon the child will be entering into adolescence, when the reins of control are transferred to himself. But now he is in the hands of those who mold him. Horace Bushnell even felt that more was accomplished for the moral and religious life before the beginning of language than during the remaining years of minority. His statement is somewhat extreme but suggestive and thought-provoking.

The home likewise has the child *longest*. Out of 8,766 hours in the year, we may say that 100 or more, on the average, are spent in church, 1,000 or more in school, and 7,500 under home direction. Taking off 3,000 for sleep, there still remain about 4,500 hours under home influence, or possibly forty-five times as much as the church gets and nearly five times as much as the school gets. The home has the child before he goes to school, during public school years, and often afterward. It has him vastly longer than the college, and with the growth of municipal colleges the time at home is increased. So, from the sheer standpoint of time, the home has a tremendous advantage over other agencies. Potentially it has a wonderful opportunity to shape character.

The home furnishes the *richest environment*. Within its

circle come birth, marriage, and death, the most significant experiences in life. Conversations about the dining table and fireside cover the widest range—family traditions, current events, daily activities, people, and conditions generally. Poverty, illness, separation, and other experiences are felt most keenly in the home circle. Tasks, achievements, and future plans are discussed freely. Love, joy, sympathy, and sorrow are realized more fully here than anywhere else. There is a sharing here experienced nowhere else. Obligations and responsibilities, especially when "chores" are assigned, are developed through the home. Because of all of these things, the home lies nearest the heart, is "the institution of right affections," and is most influential. Though Lincoln's mother died when he was ten, he said, "All that I am or hope to be I owe to my mother."

2. Handicaps

Along with the advantages of the modern home for Christian character building, there are several handicaps. One of these is its *dissolution*. In 1880 one in every twenty marriages was legally dissolved through divorce. By 1940 the ratio had reached one of each eight. Recently it has approached one of every five. In San Francisco it has been one of each two. In Tarrant County, Texas, the home of Southwestern Seminary and two Christian colleges, there were for two years more divorces than marriages. This situation creates a real problem. Hundreds of thousands of children are affected annually. Their lives are queered, and a large percentage of juvenile delinquents come from this group. So a great many homes, instead of being helps in character building, are actually handicaps. In many orphanages a large percentage of the children are from divorced rather than deceased parents.

Another difficulty is *absenteeism*. In an increasing number of homes both parents are working. In 1870 one sixth of the women were working. By 1910 it was one fifth. In 1940 one fourth, and in 1955 one third. About one fourth of our nation's mothers are working. More than two million have children under six. So a tremendous number of children spend the day with baby sitters or in homes for day care. An increasing number of children come home from school each day to find neither parent there. Naturally, this situation has its effect, consciously or unconsciously, on the character of the child. A child with absentee parents is in effect an orphan "bereft in character of a mother's love and a father's tender care." There is no substitute for parents, regardless of the other provisions made.

A third handicap is the *lack of discipline* in the home. In an earlier age parents believed strongly and practiced faithfully the old adage, "Spare the rod and spoil the child." Now, with the emphasis on the danger of frustration if the child's desires are crossed, corporal punishment has become largely a thing of the past. While corporal punishment is not the only (nor the highest) kind of discipline and can be overdone, there is truth in the quip: "One reason for juvenile delinquency is that parents in disciplining their children do not begin at the 'bottom.'" Other methods of discipline likewise have been discontinued. So character development, in many instances, has been weakened and juvenile delinquency increased. Too much freedom, money, and cars have contributed to crime.

3. Tasks

There are many ways by which the home helps greatly in the formation of Christian character. One of them is through *unconscious influence*. This includes the attitudes, the viewpoints in conversation, and the daily walk of the parents. It includes also church attendance, giving, and sabbath observance. It involves attitudes toward amusements, temperance, and other matters. In other words, it includes the whole realm of unconscious influence. This is probably greater than conscious influence; for what one is always counts for more than what he says or does. Example is more powerful than precept. Luther Burbank, the plant wizard, once said, "Surroundings act upon the child as the outside world acts upon the plate of a camera." We are largely molded by the unconscious influences that play upon us in the home. "It is by the fireside that God works out the destiny of the republic."

Formal instruction also plays an important part in the character-building activities of the home. This may be given privately, at mealtime, or in the family circle. It includes Bible reading, bedtime stories, prayer at meals and other times, and other forms of instruction. It includes, likewise, interpreting the rightness or wrongness of amusements, current activities, various moral issues, and political problems. It may well involve helping the child to understand the error and danger in the television programs he witnesses, in the picture shows he wants to attend, and in certain types of literature. Definite teaching on social and civic duties and on finding a lifework and a life partner may be given. In fact, almost every phase of life may be touched on through fireside and mealtime instruction. Guided reading may also play a very large part in the formal instruction a home offers.

Actual participation in the work of the home may be most effective. In fact, combining activity with instruction can be done better in the home than in other agencies. Here a natural laboratory is provided for expression. This can include letting the child return thanks at mealtime. It will certainly involve attendance in Sunday school and other church services. It will include also training in giving, both by enabling the child to have money of his own and by teaching him to give a tithe of it to Christian causes. Participation includes having some responsibility about the house that trains the child in a sense of obligation. The assignment of chores has a value that nothing else can equal. Likewise, discipline may be exercised in the home as nowhere else, thus training in obedience and responsibility.

II. THE CHURCH

Historically the second agency in the life of the child for moral and religious training is the church. In fact, with the development of Nursery departments to care for the babies, the church almost stands alongside the home in the matter of reaching the child first. It is, of course, the only institution exclusively for developing Christian character.

1. *Importance*

The church gets in an *early influence* in the child's life, both through its Cradle Roll ministry and its provisions at the church building. Since an increasing number of children are cared for in the Nursery departments of the church during the teaching, training, and worship services on Sunday and during other services of the week, the early influence of the church in the child's life is being intensified. When the children are in the church nursery school or kindergarten during the week, this influence is extended over more waking hours than the home has the child. So, from the sheer standpoint of hours, the church has a great influence. Thus, before the school and community have exerted themselves, the church has its opportunity. This early influence gives it a place of tremendous power in shaping the character of the child. Its approach in teaching the child is very appealing. In many ways the church is our number one agency.

The church has *distinct advantages* at several points. One is the time of meeting. This is on Sunday, a day of remembrance, rest, and worship. With many other agencies and activities shut down for the day, a certain halo attaches to the sabbath which exerts a tremendous influence, and provides a good opportunity to teach religion. Also the place of meeting is significant. With stained glass windows, reverential music, and an atmosphere of worship, an influence is exerted by the church that inevitably impresses the child. The constituency of the church is likewise influential. Here we have a group of devout people of all ages who have come together for Bible study and worship. These things give the church a place of tremendous power.

Furthermore, the church is the one institution in the life of the child that is *exclusively religious*. It is the only agency in the community that is primarily concerned with the moral and spiritual needs and interests of the people. This unique mission gives it a place of far-reaching influence. The congregation of a church exerts a tremendous power over boys and girls, not only by what it teaches but also by what it is. One never gets away from this influence. The sentiment of the song "The Church in the Wildwood" is absolutely true to life. The rich experiences of fellowship, worship, and comfort give the church a place of tremendous power. So, much of the moral and religious character of the person is formed by the church.

2. *Organizations*

The organizations and activities of the church for developing character are manifold. First, and in many ways foremost, is the *Sunday school.*

> It is the primary teaching agency of the church, and a church that neglects this function of teaching has lost something that is indispensable to its nature as a church.[2]

With efficiently organized children's departments the Sunday school starts the child off before the public school gets him, and through its provision for all ages it continues the instruction long after the college and professional schools have finished. As has been said, "The Sunday school has no alumni." Its influence is exerted from infancy through adulthood. With rich departmental programs of worship, and with classes graded as to age, aims, materials, and methods, the Sunday school is most powerful in its results. No wonder J. L. Kraft, the great businessman, said: "The modern Sunday school is the most potent factor in giving children the right start in life." And David Lloyd George, prime minister of England, stated: "All that I am and whatever I have accomplished, I owe to the Sunday school."

A strong ally of the Sunday school is the *Training Union*. It also is graded, and now provides for all ages in its ministry, with graded programs of activities. With the wide variety of topics for discussion in the Training Union programs, an individual gets a new insight into Bible doctrines, personal problems, citizenship, and missions. Also he learns to speak and pray in public. With conferences, conventions, and summer assemblies the service of the Training Union is extended still further. It is a most powerful agency in the church for developing Christian character.

The *Woman's Missionary Union,* with its departmental organizations, including the Woman's Missionary Society, the Young Woman's Auxiliary, the Girls' Auxiliary, and the Sunbeam Band, is likewise a most effective agency in the church. Especially is this true in the fields of missions and stewardship. Here again, the mission study books have been of tremendous value, as have conventions, conferences, and other activities. The Woman's Missionary Union has helped greatly in developing a missionary spirit and stewardship and service ideals. Without this organization we would still be a long way back in the woods. It has inspired all of the other agencies.

The *Brotherhood* is the last one of the "Big Four." It was somewhat slow in getting a start, finding its function, and enlisting the men; but it is well under way now. It has taken over the Royal Ambassadors from the Woman's Missionary Union and is putting new life into that organization. Naturally, boys follow the leadership of men better than they do that of women. Through local programs, conferences, conventions, and other means, the Brotherhood is doing much to develop morale and is exerting a great influence.

Gradually we are developing a system of *weekday instruction*. The Vacation Bible school is reaching countless numbers, teaching them the Bible, winning them to Christ, and training them in Christian citizenship. It has had a phenomenal growth and influence. Religious instruction on a released-time basis is gaining in popularity and influence. There is a rapidly growing trend toward church kindergartens; and in many places even the Christian day school is being provided, beginning with the kindergarten and extending into the grades and high school. The church is rapidly becoming a teaching agency to be reckoned with in the community.

The *Music Ministry* of the church is being expanded to include all who will participate. It is bearing rich fruitage in fostering Christian growth and in improving the quality and significance of music in all phases of church life. As an increasing number of churches adopt an age-graded Music Ministry, its influence will continue to expand.

In its *study course*, the church offers a comprehensive program for personal development for all age groups. The Church Study Course for Teaching and Training includes books dealing with almost every phase of Christian life and service. In fact, one can gain almost a miniature seminary training through the study of such books.

3. *Achievements*

The church gives to the child, as no other agency does, the *Christian viewpoint* of life. With the vast majority of homes having one or both parents non-Christian, the American home cannot give a large percentage of youth the Christian point of view. With the Bible and prayer largely eliminated from the public school, that agency is unable to instil the Christian viewpoint and attitude. Thus, a large segment of American youth will have to depend on the church if they ever come to see life from the point of view of Christ. Fred P. Corson well says:

> Education has a responsibility for maintaining a simple faith in a complicated life, a consciousness of divine direction in a world of tangled human relations, a comradeship with spiritual life amid the loneliness of material accumulation.[3]

The church also brings a *response to Christ*. It is the primary agency and human channel through which individuals are led to conversion. And at the heart of this task is the Sunday school. More than three fourths of the total number of baptisms each year come from that group (comprising less than one fourth of the total) of unconverted people who attend Sunday school. The main reason why Southern Baptists, during the past third of a century, have won nearly twice as many people as they had won in more than twice that time before is because of our growing emphasis on teaching. The Sunday school is our greatest evangelizing agency in reaching, influencing, and winning the lost. The discerning pastor recognizes that it is the most fruitful evangelistic field in the church.

Likewise, the church has attained great results in *Christian living*. For example, the main reason why Southern Baptists have recently given nearly twenty times as much as they did a little over a third of a century ago, with only a little over three times as many members, is that through our Sunday schools they have been trained in the art of giving and have been taught the obligation to give. Similarly, prohibition came about after a generation of teaching a lesson each quarter along that line, and if it is brought back it will be done largely through a program of teaching. The same principle is true of daily living and Christian citizenship. The church teacher is largely "the keeper of the gates of tomorrow." What we put into our teaching program today we will reap in our church life tomorrow.

III. The School

The third great influence in the life of the individual is the public school. In fact, it is the main moral factor for many who do not come from Christian homes and who do not come under the influence of church teachers. The public school is probably the greatest single socializing influence in the present-day order.

1. *Opportunities*

There are some points at which the school has the advantage over both home and church in influencing character. For one thing it *reaches all* of the children, which is not true of these other organizations. With a compulsory system of education, every child must attend a public school or one provided by some other agency. This gives the school the opportunity of helping to shape his character and makes it very definitely a determining influence in his life. It also puts upon the school system a greater responsibility than other agencies for the handling of juvenile delinquency.

Also, the school has the child for a *longer period* of time than the church. The average church has him for not more than four hours a day on one day a week, with an average attendance of not over two thirds of the Sundays. Even with a full church program the total time for the year would usually be less than four hundred hours. On the other hand, the school has him six to seven hours a day, five days a week, and for over eight months of the year. So it has a wonderful opportunity to shape his life and character, and therefore it bears a tremendous responsibility for the outcome of his life. In fact, it can practically be said that the public school is the church's greatest ally or worst handicap. Pupils simply cannot be under public school influence for all of this time without being affected tremendously by it. It is for this reason that Catholics have centered on the Christian day school.

2. *Weaknesses*

The modern public school labors under certain weaknesses in shaping the character of pupils. Often *discipline is not stressed* as it once was, or should be. Corporal punishment has very largely been discontinued, due in part to the theory of so-called "Progressive Education," which stresses the danger of frustration if the child's desires are crossed. Also there is often the opposition of parents to the school's exercise of discipline, and sometimes there are legal limitations. The result frequently is a lack of respect for teachers and a disregard of their requirements. Human nature being what it is, many pupils will not do what they should if they know there will be no punishment for violations. The result is often an insolent if not an antagonistic attitude. Joan Dunn, a former school teacher, says:

> This new methodology has raised a breed of child afraid of no one, awed by no rule or regulation. . . . He is the man of the hour and he knows it; he is conscious of his nuisance value and uses it to the fullest.[4]

Her words may be a little strong, but they are suggestive. The pupil needs to learn self-control.

Also *promotion is too easy* in many cases. Due to bus transportation, children are not usually kept in after school to make up deficient work. In many instances home assignments have been practically discontinued and, in some cases, "social promotion" has been substituted for achievement, the pupil going on to the next grade whether he masters the work or not. Some of this practice grows out of certain modern educational theories. One wonders if some of it grows out of mere convenience and a desire not to be bothered. Naturally, under lax conditions obedience, self-control, and responsibility are not developed as they should be. These conditions, of course, are not universal and exist in relative degrees. But they have given concern to many regarding the character outcome of the public schools. A prominent army psychiatrist has said it is lacking in developing discipline, responsibility, and a sense of values.

Another weakness is the *secularization* of American education. In the early days the aim in establishing public schools was definitely religious, in order that people might learn to read so they could read the Bible. Even some state legislatures gave such reasons for establishing schools. Likewise the curriculum material was religious—biblical, doctrinal, and moral material occupying a prominent place in the New England Primer, the "Blueback Speller," and McGuffey's readers. Bible reading and prayer were common in the schools. Now, many of these things have been reduced to a minimum.

A study in the Congressional library revealed that the religious content of readers and spellers has dropped from 22 per cent in early days to 0 per cent recently; moral material, from 50 per cent to 3; while secular content has increased from 28 per cent to 97 per cent.

In some states reading the Bible and praying are not permitted. In one state the Gideons are even forbidden to place Bibles in schoolrooms; in another, trustees are not allowed to ask prospective teachers about religious affiliation; and in some cities pupils are not permitted to have a voluntary prayer meeting at the noon hour.

3. *Accomplishments*

One thing which the public school does is to *democratize people* through bringing together those of various levels of economic, cultural, and religious life in one group. As pupils rub elbows with others, they broaden their understanding, sympathies, and interests. The public school system has made a distinct contribution here, and it is our greatest democratizing agency. It provides a socializing opportunity not afforded by the home or the church. To be sure this condition furnishes a danger, as pupils from Christian homes mingle with those from the homes of bootleggers and criminals, but it also furnishes a laboratory for forming contacts and strengthening character.

Also the school curriculum helps a great deal to *broaden one's viewpoint* of life. History gives a perspective look at the developments of the past. Geography helps one to see the world in which he lives. Civics enables a person to know the workings of government. Psychology helps the pupil understand himself. Other subjects reveal various phases of life. So the student is led out in all directions in his studies. Getting the viewpoint of schoolmates during the process of studying in these fields also helps. And particularly is one enriched through contact with the various teachers he has, especially dedicated Christian schoolteachers. So, through the public school system one becomes a different character.

✿ ✿ ✿ ✿ ✿

In addition to these fundamental institutions, there are other organizations and activities in the community, many of which have hurtful effects on character. These include certain business establishments. Some are licensed by society to deal in commodities harmful to life, such as cigarettes, narcotics, and liquors. A young person may take these things as entirely legitimate and never consider their harmful effects.

Another social force is public amusements. Being too young to realize the harmful elements, the child may come to accept evil picture shows, public dance halls, and other dangerous amusement activities as being all right.

Sabbath desecration may be taken as a matter of course as he sees stores, "washaterias," and filling stations doing business on the sabbath with social approval. The same principle applies to harmful television programs, crime comics, and cheap books that deal with smut. Much of our juvenile crime today is inspired by these things. The true Christian citizen must be alert to all of these influences and do what he can to counteract and curb their influence.

SUGGESTIONS FOR CLASS DISCUSSION

1. What is the greatest handicap the home faces today?
2. What do you consider the most effective phase of church work for shaping character? Why?
3. State the greatest weakness of the public school system as you see it.
4. Compare the influence of home, church, and school in the formation of character.
5. List some helpful social agencies other than those mentioned.

---

[1] Margaret Slattery, *The Second Line of Defense* (Westwood, New Jersey: Fleming H. Revell Co., 1918), pp. 66–67.

[2] James D. Smart, *The Teaching Ministry of the Church* (Philadelphia: W. L. Jenkins, The Westminster Press, 1954), p. 11. Used by permission.

[3] Fred P. Corson, *The Christian Imprint* (Nashville: Abingdon Press, 1955), p. 141.

[4] Joan Dunn, *Retreat From Learning* (New York: David McKay Co., Inc., 1955), pp. 170, 183.

CHAPTER 6

6

Life Experiences

In ADDITION TO the hereditary tendencies, innate characteristics, and influencing agencies that help to shape Christian
character, there are certain experiences that have considerable influence. In all cases, however, it is not so much what
happens to an individual that counts, as the way he responds
to it. We shall notice now some of the many significant experiences that come to people and something of their bearing on
character. Every teacher needs to know something about
these matters so as to know how to deal with the pupil, since
our teaching and training are to meet life needs. "I came that
they may have life" (John 10:10 ASV), said the Master
Teacher.

I. BODILY HANDICAPS

A considerable percentage of the population of our country
has some sort of physical handicap. About a third of a million
are blind and must adjust to life without sight. Many are
deaf and unable to enjoy the conversations going on around
them. Sometimes the handicap is a dwarfed hand or foot that
is not only inconvenient, but attracts curious attention. Scars
received in battle or otherwise may be very disturbing. Unusual size may cause a person to feel out of place with ordinary folk—whether he is a giant or a dwarf, tall or short. Even
an exceptionally high or low voice can mark a person off from
his fellows. Any physical condition that tends to set one apart
from others or to handicap his normal functioning can have
its effects. Such situations are much more common than we

realize. There are more than a million persons in our country now with some sort of handicap, and multiplied thousands are being added each year.

The most significant thing about a physical handicap is not the inconvenience caused but how the individual reacts to the problem. "Handicaps are in themselves of almost no importance; what matters is the attitudes they generate." [1] If one is able to master the handicap and go on with his life activity, no serious harm results to the personality. Many have done this and been strengthened in the process. Although handicapped by infantile paralysis, Franklin Roosevelt carried on as few men have. A mother, paralyzed from the neck down, manipulated a special contrivance with her lips to make phone calls in ordering things for the household and phoning people for parent-teacher associations and other organizations. Overcoming a handicapping condition can strengthen the person and make him a greater character than otherwise he would have been. Here is where faith and courage come in.

On the other hand, such situations may give one a feeling of inferiority and defeat and cause him to throw up the sponge and quit, or to take to drink and muddle his mind to be able to "get by." Such escape measures result in a queered and weakened personality. Lying indefinitely in bed or sitting in a wheel chair can bring the most distressing frame of mind. Betsey Barton, a confirmed cripple, said:

> The paralysis creeps up into the heart and into the mind. There is no courage. The will is gone. . . . A broken heart was certainly much harder to recover from than a broken back.[2]

Such people need not only understanding and sympathy, but also encouragement and support if the life is not to be permanently depressed and weakened. With proper backing, they can make their handicaps become steppingstones rather than stumbling blocks in forming character.

II. Health Conditions

From the *negative* point of view a number of people experience some sort of physical ailment much of their lives. Sometimes it is liver trouble which keeps them in a more or less pessimistic frame of mind much of the time. Sometimes it is a type of headache that causes suffering and a very unpleasant feeling. With others it is chronic indigestion or at least the inability to eat certain things. Arthritis causes many people to suffer much of the time. Tuberculosis still requires many to live in a certain climate. And cancer casts a shadow over the lives of multitudes.

Diseases that have some element of permanence grip the lives of many people much of the time and bring quite a bit of gloom as well as suffering. Naturally the outlook on life is changed and, in frequent instances, people take to drink or dope or even commit suicide because of these conditions. Those, however, who handle the situation positively are made stronger by doing so. Often it is the sadness of the singer that makes the sweetness of the strain. Fire does burn out the dross. Character can be enriched by illness and suffering.

In many instances there are mental difficulties that have their bearing on character. One type is neurosis. The neurotic may be in good physical health and be able to understand clearly, but still be emotionally disturbed. As someone has said, he knows very well that two and two make four, but still he is worried about it. He is likely to be anxious, fearful, and pessimistic. Properly handled, however, this trait may add strength to his character.

Along with neurosis is psychosis, in which the intellectual faculties are impaired. Sometimes it takes the form of an extreme sense of importance coupled with a feeling of not being appreciated. At other times there is a feeling of elation followed by one of depression. Occasionally there is a split personality, the individual crying when he should laugh and laughing when he should cry. If caught early enough and given competent treatment, this trait may be handled and the person be helped to a well-adjusted life.

In discussing the bearing of health on personality the *positive* as well as the negative side should be considered, for along with those who suffer from some sort of physical or mental difficulty there are others who are relatively free from these conditions. They have no physical defects or deformities. Their health is good and their digestion splendid. A good physical condition enables one to face life in an optimistic and radiant fashion. It does something positive to the personality. Similarly, when there is good mental health and the individual can feel right and face life rationally there is a wholesome outlook and attitude toward life, which is most helpful.

So health conditions, whether good or bad, have a very definite bearing on the life and character of the individual. It is therefore most important for a person to be on his guard at this point. Likewise it is very important for those who deal with him to understand the condition of his health. The recent emphasis on both physical and mental health is a valuable one.

III. PARENTAL SITUATION

The *abnormal* situation faced by a child with regard to his parents may have much to do with his character. The youngster who finds out that he has been born outside of wedlock is liable to have his life considerably queered and to fight against the situation. This problem may be faced even by children adopted into splendid homes, when they find out the real facts. There are close to a quarter of a million youngsters born outside of wedlock each year in the United States, or about sixteen million in the lifetime of the average individual. The knowledge of such a birth may lead the child to set himself against society and join the ranks of juvenile delinquents. Teachers need to be alert to counteract such results.

Another difficult situation is that faced by the orphaned or semiorphaned child. To know that one's parents are dead is quite a blow. But it is much worse to come from a broken home, as many of the boys and girls now in our children's homes do. Statistics seem to show that broken homes are one of the chief causes of delinquency. Naturally, in such a situation there is not the memory of parental love and care that is found in orphans from the normal home, but rather memory of dissension and strife. There are now in the United States as many children from broken homes as there are people in Arizona, New Mexico, Oklahoma, and Arkansas. The warped experience of the semiorphaned child tends to develop a resentful spirit and to have its harmful results on character. Here again is an opportunity and a need for careful guidance on the part of the teacher.

In contrast with the child who faces life in an abnormal home situation, there is also the child from the *normal* home with both parents living. Here he has both a mother's love and a father's care. This is the ideal situation. It represents the average home in America. Be it ever so humble there is no place like it. By and large, the home exerts the greatest influence of any agency in shaping Christian character. If the right example is set, the right influence exerted, the right ideals held up, and the right discipline exercised, the home can indeed be the cornerstone for building national character. Teachers should work toward the goal of "A Christian Home for Every Child."

IV. Environmental Influences

The *residential area* in which the individual grows up has much to do with his character. Slum sections of large cities are notorious for filth, drink, and immorality. Benjamin Fine in his study of delinquency found a close correlation between the environment and crime. He says: "The greatest evidence of juvenile delinquency is found in neighborhoods of bad housing and overcrowding." [3]

In one leading Texas city it was found that nearly two thirds of the juvenile delinquents came from a district comprising only one third of the city. The youth from the other side of the railroad tracks has one count against him to begin with. In an environment of drinking, stealing, gambling, and immorality, it is little wonder that a youngster grows up to be a delinquent. In such situations it is much more difficult to "shun the very appearance of evil" than it is under advantageous environment. So social reform goes hand in hand with personal regeneration in the work of character building.

Over against the slum areas are the better residential districts. In the suburban territory, with good homes, schools, and churches and with fewer saloons, gambling places, and houses of ill fame, youth grow up with a much smaller percentage of crime. Delinquency is greatly reduced and a better type of citizen is produced. This condition helps to explain the exodus of well-to-do families from the downtown areas to the suburban areas. In fact, in some cities in the North the white population in the incorporated areas has actually decreased in recent years. In one large Southern city the better section required only one half as many patrol cars as the slum area, had only one third as many crime trials, and required only one fourth as many units of welfare agencies. So Christian character is developed best in good residential areas.

The *geographical territory* also has something to do with life and character. The urban citizen living amid the din and strain of city life is somewhat different from his country cousin in the more quiet life of the wide, open spaces. The country boy with chores to perform is kept busy and away from the "gang" and its influence. Thus, delinquency is not likely to be as bad in the country as it is in the city. Also, the individuals in the Temperate zones have an advantage over the persons in the Frigid or Torrid zones. These last may have to spend so much energy in battling excessive cold or excessive heat that they do not have much left for engaging in more worthy pursuits. So the highest level of culture, the best opportunities for developing good character, and the greatest achievements have been found in the Temperate zones. Environment does count in personality development.

V. Economic Status

The economic standing of the individual has quite a bit to do with his life and character. At the bottom of the ladder are those who are *poverty stricken*. This is the group who, from lack of skill, interest, or opportunity, are without employment much of the time; and when they do work they get only a meager amount. So they and their families are ill-fed, ill-clad, and ill-housed. They do not have the opportunities of others. They not only suffer because of being underprivileged, but they may become jealous of their more prosperous neighbors and have an antagonistic attitude toward society. This situation brings the temptation to pilfer or steal, especially among boys. Such an attitude can leave a permanent scar on the minds of youth. In fact, it is the sort of situation where the seeds of socialism and communism are sown. There is a close correlation between poverty and malicious gangs.

At the other extreme are the *well to do*. They are the ones born with the proverbial silver spoon in the mouth, and they never lack for anything. Their children do not even have to work. Every material desire is gratified, often to the extent of having cars of their own at an early age. These privileges, coupled with free time, constitute a temptation to crime. In fact, much of the juvenile crime is related to the use of cars, time on one's hands, and lax parental discipline. As a general rule, crime increases during times of prosperity and decreases during periods of depression. The parent who says he does not want his child to have to work as hard as he did may be wishing the wrong thing for the child. Affluence brings problems. There are definitely the "up-and-out" as well as the down-and-out.

In between these two groups come the *rank and file* who are neither poverty stricken nor well to do. They are what we call the middle class. They have enough to meet their needs but not enough to be extravagant. They are not wanting for the necessities of life, nor do they "splurge," as we say. They earn their living and are kept busy and out of meanness while doing so. They constitute the ballast of the ship of state and a stabilizing influence on morals and conduct. Character is more readily developed among middle-class people. The plain, common people are our greatest steadying force. They do not lack for necessities, nor are they tempted with a surplus. They are "middle-of-the-roaders" and the ones that bear the burden in church and state. They are the salt of the earth and the hope of the world. Character development has its best opportunity here.

VI. Cultural Attainments

The level of cultural development attained by the individual has much to do with his character and conduct. Central in this culture is his *school life.* This is true whether it is elementary school, high school, or college. A considerable percentage of people never get to finish grade school. Such persons are likely to be limited in their enjoyments and attainments. Naturally, lectures and better literature do not appeal to them. Movies and other cheap entertainment are more inviting, and their viewpoints are shaped accordingly. Life is lived on a somewhat lower level than it otherwise would be, and to an extent is handicapped. On the other hand, as previously indicated, the influence of a secularized system of public schools is not all that it should be, and mingling with pupils from all kinds of homes has its effects. Our school system has a tremendous influence in many ways on character. Especially valuable is the influence of a dedicated Christian teacher.

What applies to formal schooling also applies to *reading habits*. The person who is fairly well educated will be more interested in good literature and will build up a library accordingly. Good books will add to his cultural development, will develop further insight into life, and will strengthen his character. On the other hand, the individual with a low cultural development is likely not to do much reading on his own. He is somewhat like the backwoodsman, who, when asked by a visitor what he did on long winter evenings, replied, "Sometimes I set here and think, and sometimes I just set." If such persons do read, the books are likely to be the cheap, cellophane-bound type of novels that abound in the sensational and the suggestive. The magazines read will be of the same general type rather than those that are cultural and character building. Thus life will be affected, for we can almost say, "As one reads, so is he." Herein is the value of church libraries.

Along with reading should be mentioned the matter of attending lectures of various kinds and broadening one's horizon accordingly. Likewise there is the need of selecting the right kind of programs on radio and television.

Another cultural activity is *travel*. In the horse-and-buggy days it was not easy to get far from home. Today, with automobiles, good roads, and more money, people can tour the country almost at will and can see all parts of the nation in a brief time and at moderate expense. Travel helps one to realize how the rest of the world lives and to have his interests broadened.

In this connection might also be mentioned the attendance upon conventions, conferences, and assemblies, which likewise has a tremendously uplifting influence. Ridgecrest,

Glorieta, the state assemblies, and summer camps and conferences have gone a long way in changing the lives of our people. And trips to foreign lands are most enriching. Travel has a definite bearing on character.

VII. RECREATIONAL ACTIVITIES

Recreation is one of the most important factors in the life of the individual. It is very true that what one makes during his hours of labor goes into his pocket, but what he spends during his hours of leisure goes into his character.

Recreational activities include *games*. Benjamin Fine, who questioned 1,500 delinquents, felt that the lack of recreation centers, particularly in the underprivileged sections of the city, was one of the factors contributing to crime. With properly organized and supervised games, youngsters are taken off the streets, their gang spirit is satisfied, and wholesome outlets are furnished for their energies. The YMCA has rendered invaluable service. The Boy Scout and Camp Fire organizations have rendered even more valuable service. Very few Scouts have been convicted of crime. The RA and GA organizations have also helped. Organized and supervised recreation in our churches is one of the most helpful developments we have made. As we foster in church, school, and community the right kind of recreation, we shall go a long way toward solving the problem of delinquency and developing Christian character. People who play together learn to live together. In one town a church program of recreation practically emptied the dance halls. Such a program definitely makes for character.

Another phase of recreational life affecting character is the *movie*. Many are cheap and accessible, especially the drive-in type, and are patronized daily by multiplied millions of people of all ages. It is claimed that nine million public school pupils attend movies each Saturday. Combining the visual with the dramatic, the movies are attractive and impressive. With their emphasis on sex, drinking, and crime they are most dangerous. Many juvenile delinquents admit that they get the suggestion and technique for crime from the movies. Even a boy who shot a neighbor said, "That is the way they do it in the movie." Case after case could be given where the youth followed through in his crime the suggestions given on the screen.

Closely related to the movie is *television*, which comes into the home circle before the child is old enough to discriminate. In fact, a number of movie films are given on television, with the accompanying emphasis on cigarettes, beer, and liquor advertising. Children are imbued with the spirit by the time they are able to talk, and want their mothers to buy beer at the grocery store because it "tastes so good," or they want to smoke cigarettes because they are "so cool."

Comics are another significant source of entertainment and greatly affect character. They can be bought for a very little, exchanged or traded at school, and their use is widespread. Within a decade, crime comics have increased from about one tenth of all comics to more than half. This is a tremendous increase. Fredric Wertham in his remarkable book *Seduction of the Innocent* says:

> A billion times a year an American child sits down to pore over a comic book. . . . The atmosphere of crime comic books is unparalleled in the history of children's literature. . . . It is a distillation of viciousness.[4]

Wertham gives case after case in which youngsters have carried into action the details of drinking, robbery, and murder portrayed in the crime comic books. There needs to be a ban on such materials. The thought too often becomes father to the deed. Solving this problem would help greatly to handle juvenile delinquency and would make for Christian character.

VIII. Vocational Achievements

As to achievement there are two classes of people. On the one hand, there are those who, for one reason or another, have faced *failure*. Sometimes the cause is lack of training. Poor health, financial limitations, or caring for a needy parent may prevent one from getting the formal education he sought. Consequently he feels inferior and defeated. A person the writer has known felt that his inability to finish the last few months of college work was the cause of all of his failures. Yet many great leaders never had a college education. Lack of formal training need not cause defeat.

Other persons have been disappointed in love. The loved one may have died, broken the engagement, or gone away to war and never returned. In any case there was disappointment. And often the person has not been able to center the affections on another. So there is the sense of irreparable loss and difficulty in adjusting to it.

Also, there are those who have not achieved the vocational standing or results they desired. One may not have found the proper work or may have felt the odds were against him or otherwise have been unable to succeed. Thus life is handicapped.

On the other hand, there are some persons whose every effort is crowned with *success*. They go after what they want and come back with it. If it is in the educational sphere, they finish college and professional school, whatever the odds against them. If in the realm of love, they win the girl they set out to get, in spite of the other suitors. If it is a business venture, they make good regardless of the competition, and whatever they touch turns to gold. In the professional world they climb to the top of the ladder, and in the entertainment field they are the centers of attraction. In other words, success is habitual. It is easy to see that this type of person acquires the habit of success, with the confidence, if not egotism, that goes with it. The average person may not win so regularly, but he usually comes out ahead.

There are at least three *attitudes* one may take toward life's situations. One is to see the difficulties and let them get him down until he throws up his hands and quits, or takes to drink to drown his troubles. Another is to become so absorbed in material interests as to forget weightier matters and thus dry up spiritually or become a skeptic. A third attitude is to use stumbling blocks as steppingstones and through achievement become stronger in character and service, as men like Kraft and LeTourneau have done. In any case one needs to remember that it is not what happens to him, but how he takes it that counts. With God's help we are the architects of our fate. Either failure or success may be used to strengthen character. "Underneath are the everlasting arms" (Deut. 33:27). "I can do all things through Christ which strengtheneth me" (Phil. 4:13).

SUGGESTIONS FOR CLASS DISCUSSION

1. What do you consider the worst bodily handicap one can have? Why?
2. What do you consider the most harmful environmental influence today?
3. Name some prominent characters who never finished college.
4. State some dangers of the picture show and television.

---

[1] Louella Cole, *Attaining Maturity* (New York: Rinehart and Co., Inc., 1944), p. 135.

[2] Betsey Barton, *And Now to Live Again* (New York; Appleton-Century-Crofts, Inc., 1944), pp. 14, 27.

[3] Benjamin Fine, *1,000,000 Delinquents* (New York: New American Library, 1955), p. 62.

[4] Fredric Wertham, *Seduction of the Innocent* (New York: Rinehart and Co., Inc., 1954), pp. 94, 157. Used by permission of publisher.

CHAPTER 7

I. SINCERITY

II. OPTIMISM

III. CONVICTION

IV. COURAGE

V. CO-OPERATION

VI. FRIENDLINESS

VII. SYMPATHY

VIII. KINDNESS

IX. LOYALTY

7

Personality Resources

THE TERM PERSONALITY is sometimes used to differentiate human beings from animals, meaning in that usage self-consciousness and self-determination. Occasionally it is used in the sense of individuality, or that which marks one off from others. Frequently the term has reference to appearance, as when we speak of someone's having a good personality. In this discussion we are using it in the sense of the total self, with particular emphasis on qualities that make for strength of character and furnish the resources that will help an individual meet life's problems and difficulties.

We are not stressing the physical aspect of personality, although that is very important. Vitality is a valuable factor in personality. The deformed or sickly person is handicapped to start with. One suffering from ulcers, indigestion, or headache cannot be his best self. Likewise, personal appearance is important. Cleanliness and neatness always count. A bathed face and hands, a haircut and shave, and a cleaned and pressed suit help tremendously. Necessarily there must be regard for the physical if one is to be at his best. However it is the nonphysical that is most important, particularly that which has to do with character. It is in this area that one builds up his moral bank account on which he can draw in times of need.

I. SINCERITY

A most important quality in a good personality is sincerity. The word carries the thought of being pure, unmixed, or unadulterated. In the genuinely sincere person there is no pretense or show; he is in reality what he is in appearance or what he claims to be. Honesty is at the very core of the idea of sincerity. One cannot pretend to be one thing and do another if he is sincere. His word must be as good as his bond. Dependability is also involved in sincerity. People are to be able to count on what one says or promises. Deception is out. The window must be clear if the light is to shine through.

An interesting illustration of the thought is found in McGuffey's *Third Eclectic Reader*, in his famous story of the wolf. A boy was guarding sheep near a village. He was told to call for help if there was any danger. One day, in order to have some fun, he cried out, "The wolf is coming!" The men came running with clubs and axes to destroy the wolf, but saw nothing and returned home. The same thing was repeated the second day, except that fewer men came. On the third day the wolf came, but when the boy called for help no one responded. The wolf broke into the herd and killed many sheep, including one that belonged to the boy himself. The story concludes with the statement: "The truth itself is not believed, from one who often has deceived." [1]

So it is evident that people will not long trust one who is insincere. They will not believe in his promises. In fact, sooner or later he will lose confidence in himself. It is because of insincerity that men lose out in political life. They make promises they never intend to keep, and ultimately the citizens turn against them. The same is true of political parties. Insincerity undermines the very foundations of a political party and causes the voters to turn away from it. There is no more valuable personality factor than that of sincerity. It wins admiration even from one's opponents. It is absolutely essential to Christian character. Moreover, sincerity gives the individual both a sense of release and a feeling of value.

II. Optimism

One of the most undesirable traits in any personality is pessimism. The one who is always looking on the dark side of things, seeing the hole in the doughnut rather than the doughnut itself, and painting a gloomy picture, is an undesirable character. All of us have troubles enough of our own without having those of others saddled upon us. "Weep and you weep alone" is rather true to life. No one cares to associate with a professional grouch. Whether constitutional or acquired, pessimism makes one an unpleasant companion whom people shun almost as much as they would a person with a contagious disease. There is enough gloom in the world without anyone adding to it. Throwing cold water is a thankless job.

On the other hand, we enjoy the fellowship of one who radiates optimism and enthusiasm wherever he goes. His presence is always desired. He is welcome in any gathering. He gives assurance and stimulates a following. People will rally to his leadership. Billy Sunday's campaign song, "Brighten the Corner Where You Are" struck a responsive chord. After losing a debate because he looked so sour, Henry E. Tralle resolved, "I am going to learn to smile even if I have to paint a smile upon my face until it gets to be natural." [2] And he learned it so well that, in his field work, a railroad president gave him 1,000 miles of free transportation to promote a young people's conference he was fostering. Things being as they are, most people need a lift up rather than a push down. Cheerfulness and enthusiasm are most helpful attitudes. "The man worthwhile is the one who can smile when everything goes dead wrong." If he cannot smile he can at least grin.

An optimistic disposition is a compound of several ingredients. It includes confidence and enthusiasm. Temperament enters into it, some individuals being by nature radiant personalities, while others are pessimistically inclined. Good health also plays an important part. A person with a torpid liver has a hard time being optimistic, while one with good digestion is rather naturally so. Faith in God and his cause will help to keep one confident, for he can say: "I do not know what the future holds but I know who holds the future." Trying to see the good in people and causes will promote optimism. "Many of the richest rewards of life, material as well as spiritual are never acquired simply because they are not asked for," says Douglas Lurton.[3] Counting one's blessings instead of adding up his losses will go a long way toward developing a radiant disposition. "Everyone loves a lover."

Over and over the biblical writers emphasize the importance of rejoicing. Some form of the word "rejoice" occurs over 280 times in our King James Version. Over three hundred verses speak of gladness or joy. God's word to his people through Moses contains many commands to rejoice before the Lord. "And thou shalt rejoice in every good thing which the Lord thy God hath given unto thee" (Deut. 26:11). The note of rejoicing occurs again and again in the Word of God, "Let thy saints rejoice in goodness" (2 Chron. 6:41). "The joy of the Lord is your strength" (Neh. 8:10). "Be glad in the Lord, and rejoice, ye righteous: and shout for joy, all ye that are upright in heart" (Psalm 32:11). "Rejoice in the Lord alway: and again I say, Rejoice" (Phil. 4:4). Evidently, God would have us know that joyousness is a very important personality resource and a means of glorifying our Lord.

III. CONVICTION

One must never be so perfectly poised as to hold to nothing. He must discover the facts, make up his mind, and take a stand. Otherwise, he is like a leaf blown by the wind, or a ship carried along by the waves. It is the proverbial lack of conviction that gives the politician a bad name. In order to keep the good will of all he stands for nothing, as did the man who, when asked his opinion on an issue, said, "Half of my people are for it and half against it, and I am for the people." A person without conviction is like a ship without an anchor. No one likes the individual who is wishy-washy and always agrees with the last one he meets. In fact, he cannot have the proper respect for himself.

Conviction means that a person has come to a conclusion on an issue and taken his stand. He knows what he believes, why he believes it, and is willing to stand for it. The winds of opposition, criticism, or ridicule cannot move him. When a minister visiting in a home heard one of the boys say to another regarding a matter, "But that is not right," he told the father he need have no fear for that boy. Conviction gives one something positive to hang on to. There is no trait of character more admirable. The winds of opposition may bend the one with conviction, but they do not shake him loose. Conviction is the stuff out of which heroes and martyrs are made. It is of the very essence of character.

The world sooner or later rallies to the banner of the man who has conviction. Columbus discovered America, Washington led the colonies to independence, and Lincoln freed the slaves, largely because of conviction. One reason so many professed Christians, and sometimes even religious leaders, lose their influence is that they do not stand out against the moral evils that threaten society. We admire and trust a person of conviction, even though we may not agree with him. In the days when the state legislatures elected United States senators, the Kentucky Legislature returned Henry Clay to the Senate, at the same time disapproving some of his policies. They believed in the man who said, "I had rather be right than be President."

IV. COURAGE

Along with conviction naturally comes the matter of courage, if one is to carry through against odds. One person said he liked a rooster because he not only had a crow but had spurs with which to back up his crow. Courage is the quality that enables one to stand up against the evils of the day when all around are bending to the lower standards of the hour. It helps one to go alone when his closest friends go the other route. It enables one to face criticism, ridicule, and opposition. Courage gives backbone and grit. It puts iron into the blood to meet emergencies. Nothing is finer than the courage of one's convictions. Really great characters are always courageous.

Courage is greatly needed today, with the forces of evil as brazen as they are. The liquor people even give sacred names to their products, quoting the Scriptures, using religious pictures in advertising, and putting the Christmas story on television. Crime comics and salacious, paper-bound books by the million put wrong ideas into the minds of youth and contribute to intemperance, immorality, and crime. So somebody needs to speak out, especially when these evils are increasing faster than the population. Somebody needs to speak out about the danger of the nation's going continuously into debt and facing bankruptcy, if not socialism. Courage both requires character and strengthens it.

All of the great reform movements of history have been carried forward by men of courage. It took courage as well as faith to enable the Old Testament leaders to carry through their purposes in subduing kingdoms and working righteousness. The same quality was needed in New Testament times and has been needed ever since. When General Petain faced the seemingly insuperable odds of the German army, he simply said to his men: "Courage comrades, we'll get them." And they did.

"I looked down into my open grave," said Senator Edmund G. Ross as he broke with his party, voted against the impeachment of Andrew Johnson, and lost his seat in the Senate. His deed has been called "the most heroic act in American history, incomparably more difficult than any deed of valor on the field of battle." [4] We need more statesmen like that in a day when we have become accustomed to seeing compromises on moral issues.

V. Co-operation

Some people are so constituted as to find it difficult to work with others. They are what might be called soloists. They prefer to work alone. Teamwork is out of the question. They do not like to have anyone telling them what to do or how to do it. Such persons cannot join others in a co-operative enterprise, and therefore handicap themselves and their associates. They are the lone wolf type, the extremely individualist, not fitted to be leaders or followers. They are somewhat like the old mule in the pasture, keeping in the general neighborhood of the herd, but staying a reasonable distance away. Sometimes a lack of co-operative spirit is evident even in prominent religious leaders.

While each person should retain his own individuality and independence, yet he should learn to do teamwork, even with those he does not like. In a democracy this is essential, whether in the industrial world, the professional world, or elsewhere. Home, church, school, and society all require a certain amount of co-operative activity. Within limits, every one must learn to subjugate his own interests to those of the group. In union there is strength. A father seeking to impress on his sons the value of co-operation took a bundle of sticks bound together and asked his sons to break them. They could not. Then he unbound the pack and broke the sticks easily one by one. Thus he emphasized to his sons the truth that no one could harm them if they stayed together.

So it is in real life. We must learn to give and take and work together. No one can have everything he wants. All working together can accomplish what all working separately cannot do. This principle is seen at its best in times of war, but it applies in times of peace. Football is a good illustration. The ability to do teamwork is a most important requisite of every citizen, and it can be cultivated. A little child from a home with no brothers or sisters had a terrific time adjusting himself to the group on his first day in school. When his teacher expressed her sympathy he said through his tears, "I'll get used to it." So he would. And he would be a stronger character for having done so.

VI. FRIENDLINESS

We do not live apart from others. Whether we like it or not, we are social beings. It is, therefore, very important to develop qualities that have outreach, particularly to those in need. Friendliness is necessary not only for others but for our own character and happiness. Individuals should not live as "hermit souls . . . in the place of their self-content," but rather each in his "house by the side of the road" as a friend to his fellow men. The art of friendliness has been characterized as the master passion. It is the outreach of one soul to another. Christianity in its fullest sense cannot be lived in isolation.

Friendliness includes loving people and letting one's heart go out to them in a friendly sort of way. It does not necessarily mean the back-slapping attitude of the salesman or politician, who may be interested in others for what he can get out of them. Rather, it means that quality in one's life that goes out toward others in cordial fashion because of what they are and because of one's genuine interest in them. Friendliness carries the idea of cordiality or sociability, with perhaps even a little more of the element of warmth than these words suggest. It is a warmhearted outreach to all classes, conditions, and colors. It is one of humanity's greatest needs today.

Such a quality is worth an infinite amount both to oneself and to others. A man has made a million dollars largely because he loved people and greeted them warmheartedly. Persons have made safe contacts with secluded savage tribes mainly because of their genuinely friendly attitude. Many people, because of temperament, lack of culture, or life conditions, are inclined to withdraw from others, and it requires genuine friendliness to get real contact with them. "Down deep in his heart every one is lonesome." There is no substitute for friendship. It can spread happiness to the right and to the left. Civilization itself is largely of the heart. The attachment of David and Jonathan is a classic example of the beauty of friendship.

VII. Sympathy

Going a bit further in our relationship with others, we reach the stage of sympathy. The word comes from two Greek terms, one meaning "to suffer" and the other meaning "with." Literally, then, "sympathy" means to suffer with another. Just as tears come in one eye when the other eye is affected, so one person suffers with another when the other experiences difficulty. Sympathy is a most vivid expression of one's outreaching interest in the welfare of another. Perhaps it is seen at its best in the social settlement worker and the foreign missionary. Sympathy is primarily in the realm of the emotions rather than in the intellect or will, although it may influence the latter. It is an outreach of the social urge, carrying one further than sociability or friendliness, even to the point of love.

Sympathy is not the same as pity. Sympathy must be based on respect for and acceptance of another. It is the grace which enables us to weep with those who weep and rejoice with those who rejoice.

Genuine sympathy is very much needed in the world today. There is so much poverty, disease, suffering, and sorrow that there is a tremendous need for people to reach out to others in a sympathetic attitude. Failure to attain one's goal, seeing the thing fail that one gave his life to, losing a loved one, and many other experiences, bring situations where sympathy is needed. There are multiplied thousands of children made orphans every year and there are hosts of blind people in the nation. All people some of the time and some people much of the time are in need of having this grace extended to them. The world would be a dismal place without sympathy.

Sympathy is developed as one is able to put himself in the place of another and see things through the other's eyes. In fact, the expression, "Put yourself in his place," is a good Christian motto. It will help one greatly to appreciate the handicapped and the shut-in. A great deal of the hardship in the world is due to a failure at this point. And much of the charity and help given the unfortunate grows out of sympathy. Jesus even reached out and touched the decaying flesh of the shunned leper. He suffered with him. We would do more if we sympathized more. And the one who extends sympathy as well as the recipient is enriched. Sympathy humanizes and softens life a great deal. It is one of the most needed and helpful of the Christian graces and a vital factor in Christian character.

VIII. KINDNESS

A most valuable element in character is kindness. This carries one a step further than friendliness or sympathy. It leads him to go beyond the call of duty and respond to need whatever the type and wherever found. Kindness adds the gentle touch to the sympathetic spirit. It is this trait which led Jesus to heal the blind, cure the sick, and cause the lame to walk. It led Albert Schweitzer, the missionary physician, into Africa. This spirit causes the cultured Christian to leave the comforts of a good home and community and live in an underprivileged section of a city so as to help needy people, as Jane Addams did in Chicago. Legend has it that Lincoln once stopped on a journey to retrieve a pig stuck in the mud, saying afterward that he could not have slept that night had he not done so. It was not his beauty, culture, or scholarship which made Lincoln world famous, but very largely his kindly spirit.

Kindness transcends cultural levels and leads the most intelligent to help the most ignorant. It goes over economic barriers and causes the wealthy to help the poverty stricken. It transcends racial differences, as when the kindly white man who owned a plantation shared his goods with the Negro servants. It forgets differences and antagonisms, as when the American soldiers in the Orient divided their candy and gum with the children of the very people they were fighting. As has been said, "One touch of kindness makes the whole world kin." It cements human ties everywhere. If there is ever to be world peace, it will come largely as this spirit spreads among all of the nations. Kindness has a remarkably democratizing influence.

As in the case of sympathy, kindness helps both the giver and the recipient, relieving the need of the latter and giving a sense of satisfaction to the former. It both develops character and gives support to the needy. It is an unusual grace that does both of these at the same time. More than we have realized is wrapped up on the admonition of Paul, "Be ye kind one to another" (Eph. 4:32). Kindness is a remarkable grace in a world of need. As has been said, "There are so many ways that wind and wind, when only the art of being kind is all this old world needs." There just is no adequate substitute for such an art. Everyone should seek to cultivate this inestimable trait both for his own sake and for the good it will do to others.

IX. LOYALTY

In many ways the climactic trait in Christian character is loyalty. This means sticking by a friend or a cause to the very end. Leave that out of friendship, and two people fall apart readily. Take it out of patriotism, and one will fall down on his country. Leave it out of religion, and the keystone of the arch has been taken away. Loyalty is the bond that holds together the home, the church, the school, the nation. It means staying by through thick and thin, good times and bad, popularity and unpopularity, success and failure. It is the foundation of honor, the guarantee of stability, and the assured basis of progress. It is not only a most valuable but also a most needed trait.

Loyalty, according to Josiah Royce, is the "willing and practical and thoroughgoing devotion of a person to a cause." [5] It is, as he points out, a composite of several things. One is a cause to which to be loyal. Another is willingness to devote oneself to it. The third is sustained support. One cannot be loyal and be flippant, too self-assertive, or too independent. Loyalty is at the very heart of the life of the hero, the patriot, and the saint. It involves devotion, activity, and staying put. It fixes the interest outside of oneself and bids one be faithful to it. Loyalty is a sort of compound of a sense of duty, surrender to a cause, and stability of purpose. Faithfulness, steadfastness, and persistence are its very core. Loyalty is, in many ways, the highest virtue that one can have.

No trait will do much more to develop fixity of purposes than will loyalty. Hardly any other trait will do more to foster unselfishness of spirit. Nor will any trait do more to bring about stability of character. Loyalty is the very soul of honor, the basis of unity, and the assurance of peace. The great characters of history have been marked by it—Moses' carrying through to the end, Jesus' persistence down to the cross, and

Paul's faithfulness even to death. Henry Clay, Robert E. Lee, and William Jennings Bryan have been outstanding Americans who were loyal to a cause. Even those who oppose one will admire his loyalty. No higher compliment can be paid anyone than to say he is loyal to a good cause. Loyalty brings unity and peace within and service and achievement without. It is the soul of honor, the keystone of character, and the basis of progress. "Here I stand. God helping me, I can do no other," said Luther. "Be thou faithful unto death" (Rev. 2:10).

SUGGESTIONS FOR CLASS DISCUSSIONS

1. Which five of the traits discussed do you consider most important? Why?
2. List several not discussed which you think valuable.
3. Which agency does most to develop the traits you have listed?
4. List the main character traits of Martin Luther, Robert E. Lee, and Woodrow Wilson.

---

[1] McGuffey's *Third Eclectic Reader* (New York: American Book Co., 1920).

[2] Henry E. Tralle, *Psychology of Leadership* (New York: Appleton-Century-Crofts, Inc., 1925), p. 56.

[3] Douglas Lurton, *The Power of Positive Living* (New York: McGraw-Hill Book Co., Inc., 1950), p. 9.

[4] John F. Kennedy, *Profiles in Courage* (New York: Pocket Books, Inc., 1956), p. 107. Used by permission of Harper and Brothers, copyright owners.

[5] Josiah Royce, *The Philosophy of Loyalty* (New York: The Macmillan Co., 1924), p. 17. Used by permission of J. Royce, copyright owner.

CHAPTER 8

8

Moral Forces

ONE OF THE PRIMARY NEEDS of present-day civilization is a moral dynamic adequate for the increased knowledge and facilities of our times. The remarkable developments in science constitute a threat to our very existence, unless properly used. The indiscriminate distribution of knowledge about sex and other matters, without the teaching of moral curbs, creates a real strain on the power of self-control. So, both from without and from within there comes a demand for moral resources. Thomas A. Edison even suggested that we quit inventing for twenty years until we had become good enough to use properly the inventions already made. Calvin Coolidge well said, "We do not need more knowledge; we need more character."

Seductive advertising, especially of liquor, is a real menace. Television, with its stress on crime and immorality, comes into the home circle, influencing the child before he is capable of discrimination. Salacious comics and books crowd the newsstands, pouring their vile contents into millions of minds each day. What can be done to counteract these harmful influences? What is there in human nature that can be laid hold of to fortify against these evils and help the person to go straight in a crooked world? There are several inherent forces that will help in fortifying character.

As Christian leaders we do well to seek to understand and to use these latent resources. Strength to meet temptations must be built within the individual, so that he is ready to maintain moral integrity even in an evil or unsympathetic environment. Jesus prayed for his followers, not that they would be taken out of an evil world, but that they would be kept from the evil in it (John 17:15). What moral resources, existing within the individual with whom we deal, may we employ in the matter of guiding character formation?

I. Fear of Loss

Fear is a powerful force since it operates in the realm of the emotions. Also it is universal. All ages and conditions in life are influenced by fear. It differs in degree with individuals and with the same person under different circumstances. Likewise it differs in kind with various ones and with the same person at different stages in life. Fear is the emotional accompaniment of the drive for self-preservation. When one's safety is endangered, fear naturally results. So it begins early and continues late in life. Fear is mentioned in the Bible about as often as love. It is very powerful and significant and may be very valuable.

There are several *aspects* of fear. One has to do with bodily harm. A loud noise, jarring movement, or anything out of the ordinary causes fright. Illness, pestilence, famine, and war produce fear. Another aspect has to do with possessions. Property owners are likely be very sensitive to anything that will cause them the loss of possessions. Farmers fear drought, laborers being laid off, business people a depression, and all persons a fire. Fear may relate also to spiritual matters. The fear that one may disregard the sense of right and wrong until he reaches the state where he no longer has a concern about the right is a strong motive for right doing. The realization that he may reject God to the point where religion no longer makes an appeal is a stimulus to becoming a Christian. Jesus used fear as a motive when he said "Be not afraid of them that kill the body . . . : Fear him, who after he hath killed hath power to cast into hell" (Luke 12:4-5 ASV).

Fear in any of these areas may have *values* for good. Fear of bodily harm may be used to turn one against drink. Fear of venereal disease may be a deterrent against immorality. Fear of material loss may keep the businessman from selling beer in his grocery or keeping open on Sunday, if he thinks he will thereby lose good customers. Fear might stop magazines from advertising liquor if enough good people would drop their subscriptions. Fear in the spiritual realm may cause a man to turn to God if the horrors of hell are stressed sufficiently, or if the individual feels he is about to sin away his day of grace.

As Eavey says: "Healthy fear makes for caution, safeguards against danger, and provides a stimulus to achievement. The right kind of fear is a valuable asset." [1] Aristotle well said: "There are some things which it is right and noble to fear, e.g. ignominy; for to fear ignominy is to be virtuous and modest, and not fear it is to be shameless." [2] So fear can contribute to the modification of conduct and the development of character. Rightly and wisely used, it is an entirely legitimate motive.

II. DESIRE FOR GAIN

The desire for personal gain is a *universal* tendency in human life. We see it in childhood as two little youngsters in the Nursery department struggle for the possession of a doll. We observe it in middle age as a man becomes so busy in his business or profession that he does not have time for church life. And we see it in later life when a man seeks to make his last gain before strength fails. Desire for gain is evident in the agricultural realm as a man adds acre to acre until he owns a vast area. It is seen in the business world when one enlarges his plant to carry on more activity. It is observable in the professional field as a person seeks the highest position. If dominated by the wrong motive and pursued at the expense of others, this desire for gain may lead to greed, covetousness, and monopoly, such as we see in the business and political world.

On the other hand, when controlled by the right motive this desire may be *utilized* in developing Christian character, if it is given the right direction. This is what Jesus stressed both negatively and positively when he said: "Lay not up for yourselves treasures upon the earth, where moth and rust consume, and where thieves break through and steal: but lay up for yourselves treasures in heaven, where neither moth nor rust doth consume, and where thieves do not break through nor steal" (Matt. 6:19-20 ASV). The Christian worker obeys this injunction as he uses his influence and talents in winning people to Christ. Livingstone, Judson, Schweitzer, Moody, Sunday, and Graham are examples. The desire for gain is utilized by the Christian businessman who considers his money as a stewardship and uses it in promoting Christian work around the world. This is what Mr. Welch of grape juice fame has done, when he did not get to go to the mission field himself. Other wealthy businessmen have done similar things as they have used their money to build or endow churches, orphanages, hospitals, and Christian colleges. Outstanding examples of rich Christian philanthropists are Rockefeller, Carnegie, Colgate, Hardin, Fleming, and others. They have both helped others and blessed themselves. It was said even of Jesus, "For the joy that was set before him [he] endured the cross, despising the shame" (Heb. 12:2).

III. CONCERN FOR APPROVAL

Another very *strong urge* is the concern for approval. It is widespread. It starts early in life as the little child seeks the approval of parents. It is manifested in adolescence as the youth does even ridiculous things to win the favor of associates. And it is seen in adult life as people conform almost slavishly to the customs and manners of others. Concern for approval assumes a variety of forms and exerts tremendous influence. People will follow silly styles and engage in questionable conduct rather than face the disapproval of their associates. A drunken man may be seen vainly trying to adjust his tie and stand erect to appear sober. Even a cat enjoys the fondling of its mistress, and a dog repeats his stunts to secure his master's praise. Concern for approval is universal and is worthy if the standard is what it should be.

This urge has definite *values*. For the most part we think of approval in relation to others and as such it can be used to advantage. A parent may hold up the example of worthy young people in the community as a stimulus to get a child to refrain from unworthy conduct. A lover may lead her boy friend to give up questionable practices as a condition of winning her hand. A teacher may utilize the major sentiment of his Sunday school class to get a pupil with low standards to change his conduct. We should seek the approval of the best and "the final verdict of mankind." The biblical writer uses the roll call of the saints to get us to "run with patience the race that is set before us" (Heb. 12:1). Inspiring examples do help.

We should seek for ourselves as well as for others the approval of God. Mohammedans do not drink liquor because their faith prohibits it. The same is true of Buddhists. Those who claim to be Christians should have standards that meet the highest requirements of our God. The lack of such standards contributes a lot to the moral conditions we face today. Adoniram Judson, the famous missionary, had as his life motto, "Is it pleasing to God?" and settled every issue on that basis. God's pleasure is the highest sanction one can have. One of the greatest needs today is for Christian teachers to challenge youth to meet the highest Christian standards. We should seek in every area of life the approval of God.

IV. CRAVING FOR UNITY

Closely related to what we have just been saying is the craving for unity or oneness in life. It is a *universal* characteristic. Unless all of the parts of a machine are working in harmony, there is friction. Likewise, if one of the heavenly bodies were to get out of its orbit the smooth working of the planetary system would be interfered with. So it is in the human mechanism. As long as conscience and conduct work together, there is unity and peace. When they run at cross purposes, there is disunity and unrest. Conduct must harmonize with conscience or conscience with conduct, or else there is permanent warfare and a "divided self," which can lead to all kinds of problems and difficulties. We disregard this truth at our peril.

The *need* for unity is made clear in Jesus' teachings. "No man can serve two masters" (Matt. 6:24). His words, "Take no thought for your life, what ye shall eat, or what ye shall drink; nor for your body, what ye shall put on" (Matt. 6:25) actually, in the original language, carry the idea of "Do not be distracted or divided."

Lack of inner unity accounts for much of the nervous disorder prevalent today. At the very heart of modern-day counseling is the goal of leading the counsellee to find a satisfactory point of unification in his life. In this area, too, Jesus gives the secret: "Seek ye first the kingdom of God, and his righteousness" (Matt. 6:33). When one's inner life is organized around that core, all else falls into place.

What is true with regard to the relations within oneself in the matter of conscience and conduct is likewise true in his outward relations to God and man. It is difficult to live out of harmony with one's fellows. There must be a certain amount of harmony or else discord and disturbance result. One cannot always fight against God without serious results. Some individuals go over to atheism to try to get away from

God. If it is not convenient to have him in life, then he is ruled out of existence. Others take to drink or dope to drown their troubles. Many take their own lives in an effort to get away from themselves and others. So this problem of unity or oneness with God and man cannot be ignored without very serious consequences. It is involved in Jesus' emphasis on peace.

The desire for unity also has *value*. It brings to the fore the necessity of keeping life integrated. There cannot be wholesome mental health without it. Unity is accomplished, to a large extent, by keeping life keyed to a master goal or sentiment, in relation to which particular problems take their proper place. There is more wisdom than we realize in the divine admonition, "Thou shalt love the Lord thy God with all thy heart, and with all thy soul, and with all thy strength, and with all thy mind; and thy neighbour as thyself" (Luke 10:27).

As McKenzie has pointed out, "Such a master sentiment will repress no aspect of our human nature, but will be able to sweep all the innate tendencies into the service of the self." [3] Jesus showed that his life was unified around a master goal when he said, "My meat is to do the will of him that sent me" (John 4:34). Teachers should help pupils harmonize conduct with self, man, and God so as to have a unified life. "Seek ye first his kingdom, and his righteousness; and all these things shall be added unto you" (Matt 6:33 ASV).

V. ETHICAL IDEALS

Closely related to what we have been saying is the matter of ideals. As to its *nature*, an ideal is a standard or norm for conduct. It is a goal set up for one's guidance. It is a criterion for judgment. "Ideals are the highest peaks in the mountain range of human thought." The ideal is a composite of all one's thinking and study. It has in it, also, an element of feeling and value. Harkness well says: "An ideal is an idea made

dynamic through feeling. It is a regulative value-judgment." [4]
It is evident, then, that an ideal has power to determine conduct. In fact, it is perhaps the most powerful impersonal force that can be wielded for character. More than we realize, we are guided by ideals. This principle is true even of the criminal who will suffer punishment rather than betray his companions.

Ideals serve at least three *purposes*. For one thing they provide incentives for conduct. They are goals to lure us on to God's undiscovered country. As Lincoln saw the horror of slavery in the South, he registered a determination to strike it a deathblow if he ever had opportunity. Livingstone's vision of the needs in Africa had much to do in guiding him into the Dark Continent. Ideals help to channel conduct, marking off the boundaries beyond which we are not to go. Pledging to be a steward with one's means does not guarantee that one will give a tithe. His ideal of what is required in stewardship will determine the extent of his giving. Likewise, ideals help to give control to conduct. A young person will refuse to dance or drink or play cards when in a company of young people if his ideal of Christian conduct rules out these things. "Ideals are the pulleys over which we lift original nature to higher levels."

So, forming the right kind of ideals for oneself and helping others to do so are two of the most valuable things we can do. Ideals will go a long way in determining the quality of one's Christian character. Ideals helped to lead Moses through the wilderness, set Paul's face toward Europe, directed Luther in his reformational work, and guided Wilson in his efforts for world peace. Marshall Field built a great business in Chicago on the ideal: "If I will take care of my customers, my customers will take care of me." Benjamin Kidd was right when he said: "The idealism of mind and spirit conveyed to the young . . . is capable of creating a new world in the lifetime of a generation." How important for civilization it is then that we have Christian ideals on amusements, temperance, honesty, purity, divorce, and crime!

VI. Sensitive Conscience

Much has been said and written regarding conscience, but there is no uniformity of thinking as to its meaning. Some writers consider it as moral judgment, or the act of passing on whether or not a thing is right or wrong. This concept puts conscience in the realm of the intellectual and the evaluative. Such a view makes it too exclusively a reasoning process and minimizes its motivating power. Other writers put conscience more in the realm of the will, making it largely a matter of one's habit of acting. In other words, one simply does a thing until it gets to be habitual. This concept eliminates too much the element of restraint. A third view considers conscience as an instinct. This idea however, seems too general and indefinite, if not too mechanical, and does not clearly characterize the constraining influence of conscience.

The more nearly correct view puts conscience in the realm of the emotional or affective consciousness, considering it as a monitor or a sentinel that warns one to beware of the wrong and to heed the right. From this point of view, it is one's sensitiveness to right and wrong, or his sense of moral obligation or "oughtness." Thus, conscience is both a warning bell prior to an act and a punitive agent afterward, if one does not heed the warning. Conscience does not say what is right or wrong; rather it alerts one to do what he believes to be right and disturbs him if he does not do it. It warns one against doing what he believes wrong and upsets him if he does it. As Koehler says: "Conscience never acts in matters which we ourselves do not regard as authoritative and obligatory." [5] But it does pressure one to do the thing that he thinks is right.

It is evident, then, that conscience plays a most important

role in the development of character. "Two things fill me with awe and admiration", said Kant, "the starry heavens above and the moral law within." Without conscience life would be lived on a lower level, since "the world, the flesh, and the devil" exert such a tremendous influence. It tends to keep one keyed to his ideals. A person should never violate conscience, but he may well improve the standards it utilizes. Obeying it brings peace and happiness, while disobeying it results in disturbance and unrest. In fact, disregard may mean a nervous breakdown or unbalanced mind. After fifty years one man confessed a murder to get it off his mind. An escaped convict walked into a jail and surrendered, and said later that he had the first night's sleep in months. We can wisely appeal to conscience to get pupils to walk a straight path. Washington well said: "Labor to keep alive in you that little spark of celestial fire called conscience." The soul of progress is the progress of the soul.

VII. LIFE'S LESSONS

As time goes on, there are many lessons we learn from observation and experience that have a wholesome effect on character. Nature is indeed a grand old nurse. Experience is a school in which we learn, and some will learn in no other. One of the earliest lessons learned is the *inadequacy of the material*. One has only to observe to realize that. In crises we need other resources. A prominent man in a rural community prospered financially and purchased one farm after another until he owned a large area. But in doing so he neglected spiritual matters and developed a covetous, grasping disposition. When talked to during a revival meeting, he said in reference to an appeal to become a Christian, "I might serve God from fear but I could never serve him from love." His funeral was about the saddest one could attend. A lesson like that is more effective than words and not soon forgotten.

Another lesson that has a wholesome influence is the observation that we *reap as we sow*, both as to kind and degree. "Whatsoever a man soweth, that shall he also reap" (Gal. 6:7). One does not have to live long to realize this principle, both on the positive and the negative side. The one who is willing to pay the price for an education gets it. The person who lives a good, clean life wins the respect and confidence of those who know him. And the one who lives a wicked life comes to a bad end. The observations of life demonstrate the statement, "The wages of sin is death" (Rom. 6:23). The writer received a lasting impression as a youth from attending the funeral of a neighbor who had been killed in a drunken brawl, after he himself had killed a man. No sermon could have been as impressive.

Still another truth soon learned is the *brevity of life*. At most it is only a relatively few years. We see this fact demonstrated almost every week in the laboratory of life. With many it ends in childhood or youth. As George W. Truett used to say so effectively, "We have only one brief chance at life." There is no time to waste. We must indeed learn to work "while it is day: the night cometh, when no man can work" (John 9:4). The learning of this lesson will have a wholesome effect on one's character and service. "Eyes which the preacher could not school, by wayside graves are raised." Life's observations can be an effective moral force, and teachers should utilize them in shaping character.

VIII. HABIT RESERVES

The word "habit" comes from the Latin term for "have." It's *meaning* suggests, therefore, something which has one in its clutches. Habit is a fixed tendency to think, feel, or act in a given way under a given stimulus. Habit has a physical basis resulting from the connections of the nervous system. It is definitely related to the physical organism. It is likewise a part of the subconscious mind, which is the larger segment of mental life not at the moment in the center of attention. The subsconsciousness includes not only memories but attitudes and tendencies to action. These constitute a large part of our mental life and determine largely what we are.

We are increasingly *creatures of habit.* Thinking, feeling, and acting are largely habitual. We are in effect "bundles of habits." Habit has been said to be "society's most precious conservative agent." William James expressed it forcefully when he said:

> We are spinning our own fates, good or evil, and never to be undone. Every smallest stroke of virtue or vice leaves its never so little scar. The drunken Rip Van Winkle, in Jefferson's play, excuses himself from any dereliction by saying, 'I won't count this time!' Well! he may not count it, and a kind Heaven may not count it, but it is being counted never the less. Deep among his nerve-cells and fibres the molecules are counting it, registering and storing it up to be used against him when the next temptation comes.[6]

Character *results* from habits. Sow a thought and you reap an act; sow an act and you reap a habit; sow a habit and you reap a character. One may curse, gamble, drink liquor, or practice immorality until he becomes virtually a slave to the habit. This is the situation with the alcoholic. The more than five million addictive drinkers in the United States bear mute evidence to this fact. On the other hand, the development of right thinking, attitudes, and practices can be one of the greatest stabilizing forces in Christian character. A prominent, elderly layman, when asked how he came to be at church on a cold, rainy Sunday replied: "I have built up the habit of going to church, and I have to reorganize myself if I do not go." To say one gives money or goes to church from habit is to pay him a high compliment. "Train up a child in the way he should go: and when he is old, he will not depart from it" (Prov. 22:6).

SUGGESTIONS FOR CLASS DISCUSSION

1. Evaluate fear as a moral force.
2. State several moral ideals needed today.
3. Should we ever disregard the warning of conscience? Why?
4. Mention some helpful resources other than those discussed.

[1] C. B. Eavey, *Principles of Personality Building* (Grand Rapids: Zondervan Publishing House, 1952), p. 197.

[2] Quoted by Herbert Martin in *Formative Factors in Character* (New York: Longmans, Green & Co., Inc., 1925), p. 40.

[3] J. G. McKenzie, *Souls in the Making* (London: George Allen & Unwin, Ltd., 1929), p. 97.

[4] Georgia Harkness, *The Recovery of Ideals* (New York: Charles Scribner's Sons, 1937), p. 48.

[5] E. W. A. Koehler, *Conscience* (St. Louis: Concordia Publishing House, 1942), p. 8. (Out of print.)

[6] William James, *The Principles of Psychology* (New York: Henry Holt and Co., Inc., 1918). I, 127.

CHAPTER 9

9

Spiritual Dynamics

THE PRIMARY FACTOR in Christian character is religion. By this we mean, of course, the Christian religion. Real character has both its origin and culmination in God. He is the beginning and the end. "In him we live, and move, and have our being" (Acts 17:28). He is our very lifeblood and source of strength. There must be a love for God and surrender to his will if ideals and convictions are to control in a life beset by "the lust of the flesh and the lust of the eyes and the vainglory of life" (1 John 2:16 ASV). Appetites and passions from within, and examples and pressures from without, are too much for one to meet his own strength. As Woodrow Wilson once said, "Our civilization cannot survive materially unless it is redeemed spiritually." The ultimate undergirding for character is Christ.

This emphasis brings us to the climax of our study. Character reaches its highest in Christianity. As General Douglas MacArthur has said: "We have had our last chance. . . . The problem . . . involves a spiritual improvement of human character." It is either Christ or chaos. The factors which led to the fall of the Roman Empire, as pointed out by Gibbon, are all problems in our American civilization today: craze for pleasure, dissolution of the home, spending and taxes, and decay of religion. Thus, we are dealing with something very vital. We come to religion as the ultimate source of strength for Christian character. A study of ten thousand people showed "the individuals who believed in religion or attended a church had significantly better personalities than those who did not!" [1] Let us consider some of the things involved in religious experience and their bearing on character. This is the very heart of our study.

I. RELIGIOUS HUNGER

There are two *opposing views* as to the natural inclination of the individual toward religion. One view holds to an extreme emphasis on depravity, feeling that there is nothing in human nature inclining one toward religion. In effect the proponents of this view would say that naturally there is nothing whatever good about us. In other words, "We are as bad as we can be and getting worse all of the time," therefore, all of the impetus toward righteousness must come from without. Another group, on the other extreme, claims that the child is naturally a Christian and needs only be kept so. With them it is all a matter of nurture, and conversion is not necessary. In fact, one prominent religious educator even said, "Every conversion is a tragedy."

Neither of these extremes is tenable. As is usually the case, the *truth* lies in between. The little infant is neither an angel nor a demon. At the beginning he is not capable of being either, though he has the possibilities of both. For a period he is not able to think things through and come to a conclusion of his own or make a deliberate decision. The time of accountability has not arrived. The babe is subject to being led in either direction according to the environment provided, the instruction given, and the influence exerted. Here is where the opportunity of early Christian teaching comes in. Catholics have realized its value for a long time and have put their main emphasis on Christian day schools for youth. Baptists and others are realizing increasingly the importance of teaching.

Just as there are urges in life that may lead one into evil, so there are others that may incline him toward the supernatural. God has not left mankind in a purely negative frame of mind. Psychologists used to write about a specific religious instinct that brought one to God. This concept has been generaly discounted. It is too formal, direct, and mechanistic. Instead, it is felt that any of the instinctive drives, when denied their natural expression, may produce the sense of need which will lead one to reach out to the divine Power for support. If one's life is endangered, the self-preservative urge may cause him to call upon God for help. Someone has said that the nearer one got to the firing line during war, the fewer skeptics he found.

What is true relative to the self-preservative drive is likewise true of the propagative, social, power, and unifying tendencies. When any one of these is blocked, one may respond by turning to a higher power for help. So, from many angles there are pulls toward the supernatural. Truly did Augustine say, "Thou hast made us for thyself and our hearts are restless until they find rest in thee." Blind, deaf, and mute, Helen Keller, when told through sign language about God, replied: "I always knew he existed. I just did not know his name." A famous religious teacher used to face skeptics with this statement: "Down deep in your heart you know you are not satisfied apart from God." The sinner's conscience is on the side of the personal worker. "Man alone among the animals refuses to be satisfied by the fulfilment of animal desire." [2]

II. BIBLICAL SUSTENANCE

It goes without saying that if one is to know the way of life here and hereafter he must have a thorough knowledge of biblical truths. Such knowledge is necessary both in finding one's way to God and in living properly afterwards. However consecrated or zealous one may be, he cannot go much beyond his knowledge in Christian living. Zeal and enthusiasm are not enough. The Hindu bathing in the supposedly purifying waters of the Ganges River or the Mohammedan trudging his weary way over desert sands to the sacred spot at Mecca is as consecrated as the Christian. The problem is one of proper understanding. Hosea warned, "My people are destroyed for lack of knowledge" (Hosea 4:6). Professor William Lyon Phelps of Yale University well said, "A knowledge of the Bible without a college course is more valuable than a college course without the Bible."

The above emphasis is true because of what Bible truth does for human life. It prepares the way for a sane and balanced conversion and protects against a spurious one. People become interested when they know. Though fewer than 25 per cent of the unconverted people are in Sunday school on the average, more than 75 per cent of those we baptize come from that group. "The truth shall make you free" (John 8: 32). Biblical truth also gives guidance for the Christian life. It is spoken of as "light unto my path" (Psalm 119:105). If one is to walk a straight course in a crooked world, he must know the Scriptures. The great weakness of Christianity is that Christian experience and Christian teachings are not properly related to life's problems, partly because people have not been taught to see the relation. One cannot live much better than he knows how to live.

The Bible is spoken of not only as light for one's path, but also as food for his sustenance. "Thy words were found, and I did eat them," said the prophet (Jer. 15:16). The Scriptures give strength for temptation, sorrow, disappointment, failure, and other crises. Even Jesus, the Son of God, used the Bible in warding off the devil in each of his temptations. Critics of the Bible fall back on it for support in times of need. The Word of God is indeed a hammer to break into pieces the sinner's hardened heart, a light to guide the bewildered pilgrim in a darkened world, and food to give sustenance in times of stress. It should fill the mind, control the heart, and guide the feet. And it will solve social as well as personal problems. Andrew Jackson well said, "It is the rock on which our republic rests."

III. CHRISTIAN CONVERSION

The first major religious experience in the individual's life is conversion. Probably it is the greatest single one. The *meaning* of the term "conversion" literally is "to turn with or to." It is a turning of the individual from himself to God. Other terms used in the Bible to describe the experience are "born from above," "turn from darkness to light," "have life," "lost and found," and "a new heart." They describe various aspects of the experience. Probably the most comprehensive single word is "repentance," which means a change of mind involving knowledge, feeling, and will. So conversion is a rich, manifold, and significant experience, and the most important one in a person's life. It is the day that changes the world for him. It is "the experience of entering the Christian life."

While the heart of conversion is the same for all, namely, the right relation of the individual to Christ, yet in *form* or type there is quite a bit of variation. Sex, age, training, temperament, sinfulness, and expectation all have their bearing on the form the experience takes. With some individuals it is rather sudden, as in the case of the Philippian jailer; while with others it is more gradual, as in the case of Timothy. Some experience conversion without much emotion, as Lydia did; while others have considerable upheaval, as did Saul of Tarsus. In some instances the experience is more of a struggling away from sin and a bad past, while in others it is more of a reaching out toward a larger life and better future. In any case, conversion brings an inner strength and fortification for the problems of life.

In general there are three *stages* in conversion. First, there is unrest or dissatisfaction. It is characterized by a conviction of sin and of need for righteousness, resulting in a "divided self." The second stage is that of decision. After wavering back and forth, the individual reaches a point where the die is cast or the decision made. He deliberately commits himself. This step is crossing the line into the new life. And the third stage is the period of peace and calm that follows the decision. It is the satisfaction one gets from settling the issue the right way. He is indeed "a new creature: old things are passed away; behold, all things are become new" (2 Cor. 5:17).

The *peak* age for conversion experience is much earlier than it used to be. At the beginning of the century it was about sixteen years of age. Now, as a result of our emphasis on teaching and training, it is around eleven. So the Junior age is the harvest season for conversion in our Sunday schools. Many children are converted even in the Primary department. Comparatively few persons are converted after the age of twenty. All of this means that we should "strike while the iron is hot." We should take advantage of the period when the pupil is ripe for conversion and seek to bring it about in a sane way.

IV. CHURCH MEMBERSHIP

The environment in which a thing grows up has much to do with its life. This fact is seen in parks, where tropical plants are grown near those from the Temperate and Frigid zones. Those which are not in their natural habitat have to be sheltered and protected in an artificially produced environment. It is the same with animals. The polar bear would have a hard time in the Torrid Zone or the elephant in Alaska. So it is with human beings. The climate must be congenial for moral and spiritual as well as for physical growth. A slum section or a bad moral environment is dangerous for the young Christian. So, along with getting young people born again, it is important that they be nurtured in a wholesome atmosphere away from such influences as bad pictures, dance halls, and saloons.

These facts stress the need for the new convert to be brought into membership in the church at the earliest possible time following his conversion. If newborn babes must be placed in a wholesome physical atmosphere, should not those born into the kingdom be in the proper spiritual atmosphere? Not only should they come into church membership but also into membership in the various organizations of the church, such as the Sunday school, the Training Union, and one of the organizations of the Brotherhood or the Woman's Missionary Union. By this means the new convert is thrown into fellowship with other Christians and helped in living a good life. And as previously indicated, there is the value of Bible study and religious training in these organizations, all of which aid Christian development.

It is most important that a church furnish a wholesome social and recreational life for its young people. Thus, it not only helps to keep them occupied and away from evil associations, but also provides the stimulus of healthy social life. A young Christian should not have to go "off into the world" to find his entertainment. The church should provide a place and program for banquets, socials, dramatics, and other entertainment adapted to the ages and interests of the membership. It may also very well include the Boy Scouts and Camp Fire Girls. All of these organizations, in addition to the church organizations for youth, are most valuable in developing Christian character. When Theodore Roosevelt was asked whether one could not live as good a life outside the church as in it, he replied, "Maybe so, but I have never known anyone who did."

V. DIVINE WORSHIP

Worship is near the heart of developing a spiritual dynamic adequate to meet the needs of the times. As to its *nature* the word literally means "worth-ship" and has its setting in the courtroom, where the judge was addressed as "your worth-ship." So it carries the idea of reverence and regard. It grows out of the recognition of God's goodness and what he has done for us. Worship may be thought of as a wholehearted adoration of God; an outreaching of the soul for vital union with him; a definite determination to make one's character like God; and a complete consecration of one's powers to him and his kingdom.

For several reasons there is a great *need* for worship. For one thing, absorption of time, thought, and energy in things causes a person to lose sight of the spiritual and the super-natural. The stress and strain of daily life take their toll on his nerves. And, too, one is likely to become critical and un-grateful. Likewise, there is a great need for getting the mind off self and personal interests and centering it on something beyond. So worship becomes a practical necessity for re-charging spiritual batteries and enabling a person to face the strain of life. As the psalmist puts it, "My feet were almost gone; my steps had well nigh slipped" (Psalm 73:2).

> To win the great battles of personality you must organize your life through prayer and public worship around the God-given values of the Christian faith.[3]

There are a number of *values* that come out of worship. For one thing it tends to give insight so that one is better able to understand his problems and needs. Often seeming dif-ficulties are dissolved. One comes to know God and his plans better. Likewise, he gets reinforcement to face life's problems. Like Elijah, we often feel that we are fighting a battle single-handed. Worship serves as a tonic, a moral and spiritual dynamic, to meet life's issues. "They that wait for Jehovah shall renew their strength" (Isa. 40:31 ASV). There is a depth of meaning that comes through worship which one does not get otherwise. The genuine worshiper gets close to reality. "The joy we share as we tarry there, none other has ever known." [4] Worship is at the very heart of Christian experience.

There are several *aids* to worship. One is the proper atmosphere. A nicely painted, properly lighted, and tastily decorated room will help. Stained glass windows are of value. Good pictures help. Appropriate music, both instrumental and vocal, is most stimulating. Scripture reading is of tremendous value if the selections are of the right kind. Poems and other devotional thoughts may be used to advantage. Prayer is at the very heart of worship—both silent and public —especially if the latter expresses the congregations's gratitude and aspirations. Testimonies and spiritual messages lend aid, particularly if they keep close to life. Graded worship through the various educational organizations of the church is especially valuable, since it comes within the range of the experience and the interest of the participants.

VI. UNDERGIRDING FAITH

This title is used because it expresses a *need* practically everyone has at one time or another. There come times in life when the world seems to cave in on one. Sometimes it is a health problem, when sight is lost, hearing gone, paralysis strikes, or an incurable disease develops, and the individual finds himself up against an immovable wall. Sometimes it is the failure in one's undertaking, when the bottom falls out, and a person comes helplessly to the end of his resources. At other times the need arises when loved ones and friends pass away, until the individual finds himself without close acquaintances and feels the chill of loneliness. At still other times the trial comes as one nears the end of the journey, realizes that his work is about over, and feels that there is nothing much more to live for.

Under such conditions feelings of fear, despair, and uselessness can control the life. It was just such a situation that Job faced when the reports came informing him that his oxen and asses had been taken away by the Sabeans, the sheep destroyed by fire from heaven, the camels led off by the Chaldeans, and in each case the servants destroyed. Then a storm came while the sons and daughters were eating and drinking in the house, destroying the building and killing them. Finally, Job himself was smitten with boils, and his wife urged him to renounce God and die. When one's world caves in on him in such a fashion, what can he do? Some people take to drink and dope to drown their problems; others lose their minds and live in a fanciful world; and still others take their lives. Without doubt, people need supernatural undergirding.

The *sustenance* they need is found in faith in God. It is "the giving substance to things hoped for, a conviction of things not seen" (Heb. 11:1 ASV margin). It strengthens and sustains when one cannot see the outcome. Faith supported Noah as he prepared the ark for the coming flood, Abraham as he launched out into an unknown country, and Moses as he led the Israelites out through the desert. Faith supported others as they "subdued kingdoms, wrought righteousness, obtained promises" (Heb. 11:33) Even Job came out of his calamities with a new grip on God. A prominent foreign missionary, after years of seemingly fruitless endeavor, when asked about the future, said, "It is as bright as the promises of God."

"The release of power that comes with this victory of faith is the most impressive phenomenon of human experience." [5] Faith is indeed "the victory that overcometh the world" (1 John 5:4). "Underneath are the everlasting arms" (Deut. 33:27).

VII. CHRISTIAN SERVICE

To be kept busy is one of the most helpful experiences that can come to a person. It has several *preventive* values. For one thing work tends to save from temptation and evil. Most of the drinking and other dissipations come on week ends or during vacation. An idle brain is still the devil's best workshop. Christian service also saves from doubt. John the Baptist's doubt came, not when he was out in the desert preaching repentance, but when he was sitting idly in prison. Activity helps to keep one from backsliding. This is a further reason for enlisting Christians in service, since we now lose by other means than death about a fourth of those we baptize. When a little girl was asked why she fell out of bed, she said it was because she went to sleep too close to where she got in. So it is with many who join the church.

On the *positive* side, wholesome work causes one to grow and develop in the Christian life. Also it tends to keep the fires of faith burning more brightly. A church member, who wanted his name taken off the church roll because he was not fit to be a member, changed his mind when he followed the pastor's request to take gifts and talk and pray with an invalid woman. Likewise, service brings out the best in life. Many a common country boy and many a pampered city dweller found a new level of life when thrown into the heart of a world war, where service and sacrifice were called for. There is wisdom in the Master's statement, "He that loseth his life for my sake shall find it" (Matt. 10:39). Service brings the highest satisfaction.

There are many *avenues* of Christian activity. Faithful attendance on the services of the church is one. It helps others and brings to oneself a sense of satisfaction not otherwise attainable. Praying for the pastor and other church workers is an invaluable service, too often neglected. Even the shut-in can do this. Giving of one's means as the Lord has prospered is of tremendous value. "He which soweth sparingly shall reap also sparingly; and he which soweth bountifully shall reap also bountifully" (2 Cor. 9:6). This was said definitely about giving. Assuming a place of responsibility has probably a higher value still, both for oneself and for others. It may be teaching a class or superintending a department in a Sunday school. It may be leading in a Vacation Bible school, the WMU, or Brotherhood. Through such service one grows "unto a perfect man, unto the measure of the stature of the fulness of Christ" (Eph. 4:13). Attaining such growth is life's supreme task.

As has been said truly: "Fame is a vapor, popularity an accident, riches take wings and fly away, only one thing endures, and that is character." It is indeed the finest fruit that earth holds up to heaven. To have a part in forming it is a sublime task and a matchless opportunity. As we grow character for ourselves and help others to do so, we are not only working at the heart of civilization's greatest need today, but also laying up for ourselves and others treasures in heaven. May we be faithful to the task.

SUGGESTIONS FOR CLASS DISCUSSION

1. Why do we not consider religion an instinct?
2. What imagery is used to describe the Bible?
3. Give illustrations of different types of conversion experience.
4. What do you consider the most helpful part of the worship service? Why?
5. Show how work strengthens the Christian life.

---

[1] Henry C. Link, *The Return to Religion* (New York: The Macmillan Co., 1936), p. 13. Used by permission of the publishers.

[2] Ralph W. Sockman, *The Higher Happiness* (Nashville: Abingdon-Cokesbury Press, 1950), p. 94.

[3] Sterling W. Brown, *Developing Christian Personality* (St. Louis: The Bethany Press, 1944), p. 32. Used by permission.

[4] "In the Garden." Words and music copyright 1940, renewal. The Rodeheaver Co., owner. Used by permission.

[5] Blanton and Peale, *Faith Is the Answer* (Nashville: Abingdon-Cokesbury Press, 1940), p. 36. Used by permission of authors.

Questions for Review and Examination

CHAPTER 1

1. Discuss the historical evidence for heredity.
2. Differentiate between biological heredity and prenatal influence.
3. Explain what is meant by social inheritance.
4. Give four suggestions on utilizing heredity.

CHAPTER 2

5. Discuss the nature of instinctive urges.
6. Explain briefly three kinds of urges.
7. State three characteristics of instinctive urges.
8. Show the significances of urges for the teacher.

CHAPTER 3

9. Describe the physiological types of temperament.
10. Describe the psychological types.
11. Discuss three determinants of temperament.
12. State three results of temperament.

CHAPTER 4

13. Explain the handicaps of the home.
14. Evaluate the tasks of the home.
15. Name the educational organizations of the church and briefly state the purpose of each.
16. Cite some weaknesses of the public school; some wholesome contributions.

CHAPTER 5

17. Discuss parental problems faced by children.
18. Show how environmental conditions affect character.
19. Explain the significance of cultural attainments.
20. Discuss some recreational activities influencing character.

CHAPTER 6

21. State some helps in remembering.
22. Explain the types of imagination.
23. Discuss the kinds of feeling.
24. How can the teacher deal with will?

CHAPTER 7

25. Show the importance of sincerity.
26. Evaluate and illustrate courage.
27. Show the need for and development of sympathy.
28. Define loyalty and show its significance.

CHAPTER 8

29. How can fear of loss be turned to a good account?
30. How may the teacher utilize the concern for approval?
31. What purposes do ideals serve?
32. Cite some lessons we learn from life.

CHAPTER 9

33. Discuss the imagery used to describe the Bible.
34. Explain the stages in the conversion experience.
35. What are some of the values of worship?
36. State some preventive and some positive values in Christian service.

Notes